Andy Kempe

The
Script Sampler
Extracts for performance at GCSE

2
EDITION

Published in 2002 by:
Nelson Thornes Ltd
Delta Place
27 Bath Road
CHELTENHAM
GL53 7TH
United Kingdom

02 03 04 05 06 / 10 9 8 7 6 5 4 3 2 1

A catalogue record for this book is available from the British Library

ISBN 0-7487-6510-7
Page make-up by Alden Press
Printed and bound in Croatia by Zrinski

Contents

The number in brackets after each play title denotes the number of speaking parts in the extract.

Preface for teachers

Drama is flourishing in schools. Alongside the healthy traditional culture of performing plays as part of the extracurricular programme, the number of students opting for GCSE, AS and A Level courses has risen steadily over the last decade and some significant shifts have occurred in the way drama is taught and examined. Key among these is a renewed appreciation of the place of studying and performing plays as an integral part of the Drama curriculum. The National Curriculum for English and the National Literacy Strategy for Key Stages 2 and 3 both emphasise the study of how plays are written and interpreted in performance. Students are expected to study a range of plays, including two by Shakespeare in their secondary school careers as part of their work in English as well as a range of other plays representing different styles and genres. While some GCSE specifications have always offered opportunities for candidates to study and perform playscripts, others have focused more on improvisation and role-play. Now, all students taking GCSE Drama are required to study at least one full-length play which has been written and performed professionally.

Such a study presents a number of challenges for students and teachers alike. For example, students need to learn how to understand the processes involved in bringing the words on the page to life in performance. This implies not only that they must develop skills in literary interpretation and acting, but that they appreciate how performances are directed and designed and how lighting and sound technology is used to communicate meaning. The challenge for teachers often involves resources. Ploughing through a whole play is time-consuming and will, of course, only give the students access to a relatively small number of dramatic devices. The chosen play may be firmly fixed in one particular genre and demonstrate one particular style of writing. A lot more may be learned by comparing short extracts of plays drawn from different genres, times and cultures. The problem here is that the stock of plays possessed by the Drama and English departments may be quite small and there is no money to buy whole sets of new plays or even samples of a number of different plays. Even if the funds were available, teachers would then have the task of finding suitable extracts that could be used to illustrate particular points and give students the opportunity to tackle a variety of practical challenges.

When it comes to the students themselves selecting extracts of a play to perform, they will doubtless be daunted by the task of reading through a number of complete scripts in order to find something that will suit their taste and skills. Even if teachers were able to carry catalogues of plays around in their heads, it would be a tall order to expect them to be able to cross-reference the demands of casting, subject matter, genre, style and language and then be able to help different groups of students to tackle them all.

This book originated from my own frustrations in trying to find suitable extracts for students to perform as a part of their GCSE practical examinations. Inevitably, students would tend to only vaguely know what sort of play they wanted to work on and then looked to me to suggest some possibilities. No doubt like many other teachers I began to build up a collection of extracts that might suit different sized groups and present a rich and varied diet of dramatic experiences and learning opportunities. One outcome was the publication of *Drama Sampler*. This book is, in effect, a new edition of *Drama Sampler*. The original text has been revised and the choice of extracts reconsidered in the light of valuable feedback from teachers and a careful consideration of the new GCSE specifications. The publication of this re-formatted edition coincides with the release of new editions of *Starting with Scripts* and *The GCSE Drama Coursebook*, also published by Nelson Thornes. As companion volumes, the three books aim to provide students across the secondary age range with a comprehensive knowledge and understanding of how plays reflect the society that spawned them, how they work on stage, the different techniques writers use and how the scripts may, in turn, be used to stimulate new dramatic exploration.

It has been a rewarding experience to revisit this text but hard to make choices about what extracts to include – the fact is that there are so many good plays around! Nevertheless, I hope that this anthology will give you a flavour of some plays that you may not have considered using with your students before. Some of the suggestions for practical ways into the plays are designed to allow teachers and students to work together as a whole class. Other activities give students ample opportunities to take charge of their own practical investigations and produce written coursework to evidence their learning. If you, their teacher, can offer further guidance without stemming your students' own creativity then so much the better. What they can do with your help today they will be able to do on their own in the future.

Andy Kempe

Introduction

A quick look at the listings for best-selling CDs will reveal that there is a good market in selling collections of 'hits' by different artists. These collections are sometimes called 'samplers'. The popularity of these samplers isn't surprising as it's sometimes good just to be able to dip into things and get a taste of them rather than listening to a whole album. Of course, if you discover you really like the work of a particular band or singer you might be encouraged to go and buy more of their work. Alternatively, you might just enjoy getting to know a range of styles; variety, as they say, is the spice of life!

This book gathers together extracts of plays with different styles and subjects. As with a sampler album, you might get a lot from dipping into the collection as a whole or looking at one or two of the extracts in more depth. Perhaps you'll be encouraged to go away and read the complete play from which an extract has been taken. The extracts are gathered into five different categories according to the sort of emotional response they are likely to get from an audience. Very few plays will fit neatly into just one pigeon-hole, of course; perhaps the very best theatre is that which provokes a whole range of contrasting emotions, so the categories chosen here are just a quick guide and starting point.

Drama reflects, and sometimes affects, the society that produces it. Knowing a little about when a play was written and why can be very helpful in understanding the play and how best to perform it. Each extract in this book is introduced in a way that will give you an idea of what the whole play is all about and what its historical context is. The extracts themselves should last between 10 to 20 minutes in performance. After each extract a number of exercises offer the chance to explore them through discussion and practical work. The first section of these exercises will guide you to a better understanding of who's who in the piece, what's going on and why. The second section will remind you that plays are written to be staged and that what an audience *sees* the characters doing is as important as what they *hear* them saying. Finally, there are some suggestions as to how the themes and techniques illustrated in the extract can be developed into new work of your own.

What you will find over the next pages are some guidelines to help you move from reading the extracts and working on them practically to actually staging a piece of drama. If you need to choose, rehearse and perform a piece of script, or develop your own drama for an examination, you will also need to be able to describe and evaluate the process you have been through. Use these guidelines as a checklist of the different stages you go through to help structure your reflections.

INTRODUCTION

Presenting a piece of scripted theatre

To get from the initial idea of presenting a play to actually putting it on in front of an audience can be like fighting your way through a jungle. Where do you start? Where do you go next?

What follows in this section is a possible route.

To sort out a muddle you need to put your demands into an order (see page 3).

We'll need to like what we're doing.
We'll have to agree about what we like.

We'll have to be able to work together as a group
and talk to each other.

Just talking can be dull.
We'll need to get into action as soon as possible.

We won't know the words but we can use our own ideas
to keep the scene going.

We'll need to decide who's going to watch the play, and
remember them as we decide how to play the scene.

We're pressed for time and probably lack technical experience.
We'll have to keep it simple.

If we're doing a scripted play we'll need to
learn the lines and get rid of the books.

It's going to be hard but we mustn't give up.
We'll have to keep using our own ideas to solve the problems.

We'll need to have everything ready before showing it. We'll need to
know all the lines, know where to stand, have the right costumes, the
right props and know what to do with them.

We'll need to rehearse it as if an audience is really there.
We'll need to have a dress rehearsal which is as much like
a real performance of the play as possible.

When we've done it, we'll need to know where and
why it worked or failed.
We'll need to be able to build on our strengths.

INTRODUCTION

1 Set up a working notebook

• Keeping a diary or 'working notebook' of your preparations will help you in many ways. You may be required to hand in a piece of coursework which explains what you have done and how you prepared, or answer a question about your work as part of an exam. So much happens when you are preparing a performance that you simply won't be able to remember it all unless you keep notes.

• Use the chart on page 3 as a guide to the different sections of your notebook. For example, make a note of your initial discussions on what sort of work your group likes doing and what you think the strengths of different group members are. Note down how you moved from discussion into action and the different ideas people put in that helped you all move forward. Go on to keep notes of how the characters developed and what decisions you made about staging the play.

• It's a good idea to put sketches and diagrams into your notebook to record your ideas about costumes, set design and where people should stand on stage at key moments. You might also find it very helpful to take photographs of your group at work to remind you how you made the performance visually interesting. Stick these photographs into your notebook and note down the gestures and expressions people used to convey character and emotion.

2 Choose what you like best

• Don't simply decide to tackle a script because it's the first one that turns up. The most important thing a script must do is interest you. If it does this you will feel keener to work out the problems involved in staging it. Getting hold of and reading a copy of the whole play, or better still seeing it, will help you enormously in your own work.

• Students often pick a play simply because the number of people in their group matches the number in the cast. This isn't a good way of approaching the problem. It would be better to find a play you like and try to persuade people to be in it by explaining why you think it's worth doing.

3 Work as a group

• Everyone in the group must read through the extract – if not the whole play. If you try to take a back seat and just do what others tell you the whole project will quickly become very boring. If it is others in your group who aren't really involved, try to encourage them rather than criticise them – it may be that they don't wholly understand the play and feel uncomfortable with it.

• Having found an extract which seems to interest the whole group, read it through at least three times. Change the casting each time and don't be deceived into thinking that the character who has least to say must be the easiest part – he/she may be on stage the whole time, in which case they will have to be doing something; at least when the playwright has written words for the part you have some idea of what you're meant to be doing.

4   Talk through the problems

• Having read the play, make a few preliminary decisions on what it's about. The questions at the end of the extract will help you, but before tackling them you could simply ask yourself the following questions:

Who appears in this extract?
Where is it set?
When is it set?
What is the tone/atmosphere of it?
What actually happens?
What sort of people are the characters?

5   Get into action

• Avoid getting into arguments about who is going to play whom in the early stages. The main thing is to get the play off the page and into action so that you can see where the problems are and possibly discover who will be able to solve them best. At this point you may choose to have a director who will be able to tell you what the thing looks like and suggest ways of improving and developing it.

• After your initial readings, 'walk' through the play by setting up an area which is roughly where you'd imagine the play to be set. Use chairs or chalk marks on the floor to provide an outline.

6   Use your own ideas

• Put down the extracts and try to improvise the scene. Don't worry about getting the lines right – just try to include the major bits of the action and possibly a sense of what the characters are like.

• By improvising the scene like this three or four times you will begin to see how the characters relate to each other, what they think of each other and how they feel about the situation they are in. Test this against another reading of the script to see if your version of it is going in the right direction. If you have a director, she will be able to judge whether or not your improvised version really did resemble the original in any way.

7   Keep it moving

• If moving around the marked-out area seems difficult, try to act out the scene by having someone else read all the lines while you provide the actions. Without the book to distract you, you will be able to concentrate more both on your movements and facial expressions.

8 Who's going to watch

• At this point you ought to remind yourselves that a play has an audience. With a lot of plays the audience watches from one direction only. If this is the case you will have to adjust the way you are positioned so that the audience always has a good view of what is most important. As a general rule the further 'upstage' you are (that is, the further you are from the audience) the closer to the centre line of the stage you should be. If you are 'downstage' and close to the audience when others are on stage, you should be out towards the edge of the stage. This isn't a hard and fast rule, but I suggest you use it as a basis and develop it into more interesting patterns if you can. Some plays don't require an audience to watch from just one direction: they might be all around the stage (look at *She's Dead*), or perhaps on two sides of it with the acting in a channel in the middle (look at *Example*). You must decide where the audience is going to be and rehearse with that in mind.

9 Keep it simple

• Don't waste time early on in rehearsals making scenery and props which will get broken or lost. The most important thing is to be able to tell the story and help the audience see what the characters are like. Sets are not as important as what happens on them, so if you are pressed for time, keep things as simple as you can.
• You might find that one or two props are very important to a character, in which case you should rehearse with them as much as possible. In *The Golden Pathway Annual*, for example, the Headmaster's cane is almost a part of the man himself, so the actor must feel used to having it in his hand. Similarly, a costume – or, in the case of *Johnson Over Jordan*, a mask – can present big problems to an actor if he/she is not used to it.

10 Get rid of the books

• Some people can learn lines very quickly indeed. If you are one of these people, then you should start learning your lines straight away so that you can get rid of the book and concentrate on learning how to use your hands as part of the character. If you aren't so quick at learning lines you should still start trying to learn them immediately, as putting it off will only make you feel the pressure even more.
• Don't try to learn lines just by reading them through time and again. You really need to test yourself on them by turning the book over and trying to remember

them. Better still is to get someone to help you by reading the other parts and stopping when it's your turn. Lines will only come across and sound natural if they are well learnt and you are used to saying them. Similarly, it's impossible to build a convincing picture on stage when everyone is holding a book.

11 Stick with it

• The worst thing you can do when working towards a presentation is to keep changing groups or to keep changing your minds about what play you want to do. Don't start rehearsing until you feel sure that you have chosen the right play and the right group. Once you've started then stick to your decision. All projects go through a rough patch when little progress seems to be made and you've said all the lines so many times they become boring. You just have to press on and rehearse it to the point when the material becomes effective again – not for you but for someone who is watching it for the first time.

• Lights and sound effects will need to be added, but again, don't make your lives unnecessarily complicated by trying to do anything too complex. Much will, of course, depend on the equipment and experience you have available.

12 Tried and tested

• Before performing to an audience you should have a full dress rehearsal in which absolutely everything is as you want it. If a prop hasn't appeared at this stage you have no guarantee that it ever will. Treat the dress rehearsal as a performance.

• Tackling a piece of script isn't easy but it is enormously rewarding if it is a piece that you personally enjoy and feel something for. If you rush your preparations or try to take short cuts you can end up hating what you once liked. Put your own ideas in and you'll end up liking it more.

13 Evaluate what you have done

• At the end of any performance you will no doubt have a gut reaction as to how it went. You need to be able to nail down where those feelings are coming from. To go away saying 'It was great' or 'It was rubbish' will not help your future work unless you can identify just what was 'great' or 'rubbish' about it.

• Ask other people for their reactions to the work. Members of an audience will notice things you may have missed. What might be clear and satisfying to you may have confused and frustrated them. Did you really communicate what you wanted to communicate?

• Criticism is only useful if it is constructive. By being critical of yourself and accepting other people's assessment of your work you should feel better equipped and more confident about tackling future projects.

• Look back through your working notebook. If you have to hand in a piece of written coursework you will need to select what you now feel to be the most important decisions you took and talk about the effect they had on the final piece. Your notes might be very personal and sketchy – that's fine for you, but remember that someone else will need to read your coursework and make sense of what you were trying to achieve and how you went about it, so you will probably need to rewrite your notes for them.

Building a play from improvisation

1 Set up a working notebook

• Look at the notes on page 4 for guidance on how best to do this.

2 Start on firm ground

• Improvisations tend to fly off in unexpected directions once launched. The main thing is to launch them. If you can isolate, first of all, just one thing you want to concentrate on from the extract on which you are basing the improvisation, you will have a strong enough starting-point.
• Look at these suggestions of how to set up a starting point for an improvisation:
>   1 Start with a place: An office (*The Lucky Ones*) – what's the day to day banter?
>   2 Start with a discovery: A dead body is discovered (*She's Dead*) – how do people react to the discovery?
>   3 Start with a tense situation: A person has been condemned to death (*Example*) – what effect does the decision have on different characters?
>   4 Start with an argument: Two sides disagree on what's to be done (*Indians*) – how does each side put forward their case?
>   5 Start with the arrival of a new character: Someone turns up in a situation and stirs up some trouble (*Black Comedy*) – how does their arrival change people's attitudes and behaviour?
>   6 Start with a line of dialogue: 'I've been ill' (*Johnson Over Jordan*) – what possibilities arise when someone says something which seems to demand some sort of response?

Any place, character, theme, line of dialogue, incident, prop or piece of costume can be used as a starting-point for an improvisation. The main thing is to give it a go!

3   Don't talk, do

• Actually improvising on your feet will generate many more ideas than sitting around discussing what you might do. The best ideas are often those produced spontaneously. Having agreed on a starting point, it should be easy to develop the improvisation from there.

Two people sit in an attic room. Someone walks in and . . .

A dead body lies on the ground. Into the scene walks . . .

It is the night before the execution. The condemned man . . .

If you have just finished any of the above sentences you already have the basis for your improvisation. Improvisations are all about trying to generate ideas, so don't worry about ending them. The end will be when it 'dries up'. At this point sit and remind yourself of the strong elements of what you have just created. It would be useful if you could write them down or record them for future reference.

4   Develop a thread

• It is very likely that in the course of one of your improvisations you will hit upon something that immediately strikes you as being worth further exploration. Alternatively, you may want to stick to some of the other ideas in the original extract. Either way, you need to develop your improvisations until you have plenty of material from which to build the scenes you eventually decide on.

• One way of doing this is simply to take a different perspective:

Two people sit in an attic room talking about someone. Suddenly that very person walks in . . .

You are passing a house and hear shouting coming from the attic room. You know the people in there so you . . .

You are the furniture in the attic room. If only you could talk you'd be able to tell of the time when . . .

After improvising 'around' the situation in this way you may be able to see not only the drama in the original incident but how that situation developed and the implications of it for the future.

5   Make a treatment

• A 'treatment' is simply a brief incident-by-incident account of a story; it need be no more than a list of the major events of the play noting, for example, when people come in, when/why they leave and their attitude towards and effect on the others in the scene. Your story might be told in a number of short scenes or through a number of key incidents within a longer scene. Writing or recording a simple treatment will serve as a good foundation when you go on to polish the work.

6 'Go for it'

• Improvisations can go on forever if you let them. If your task is to present a piece of theatre you will have to stop adding new material at some point and shape what you have already created. You might want to try to script what you've done, but often lines which were funny when spoken spontaneously sound awful when learnt as lines on a page. Try instead to work from your treatment so that an element of spontaneity is kept.

• Refer back to the suggestions for working from a script for ideas about when and how to tackle set, props, lights, sound and the final rehearsals.

• Finally, don't worry about improvisations 'going wrong'. Their strength as pieces of theatre is that they are new and alive and therefore prone to having good days and bad days. Just because your improvisation has a few bad days don't smother it – perhaps it just needs treating with a bit more care.

7 Evaluate

• The process of evaluation is as important here as for a piece of scripted work, though there is the possibility that you will feel more personally affected by it – these are, after all, your own ideas on the line. For this reason you should be clear that what is being assessed is not so much the quality of your original idea but how well it worked in performance.

• Look back at the notes about how to evaluate on page 7.

THE EFFECT OF GAMMA RAYS ON MAN-IN-THE-MOON MARIGOLDS

by Paul Zindel

CAST (in order of appearance)

RUTH
TILLIE
BEATRICE
*NANNY

3 speaking parts. *Non-speaking part.

Gamma rays are released after nuclear reactions or when radioactive materials decay. The amount of energy they contain is highly destructive. Depending on the amount of exposure to the rays, life forms are either completely destroyed or become mutated, that is, their normal development is changed into something new and strange.

In Paul Zindel's play, Tillie conducts an experiment as part of a science competition to see what happens when man-in-the-moon marigolds are exposed to different levels of gamma radiation. What she finds is that the seeds of this bright and joyful flower which received just a small amount of radiation can still develop normally. A moderate amount of radiation causes the marigolds to change their appearance, while a lot of exposure either kills them completely or leads them to grow into small and vulnerable adult plants. Tillie wins the competition but the play raises the question of whether or not she will survive the destructive energy that she has been exposed to. In effect, Tillie's experiment is a metaphor for her own life. Like the cobalt-60 that the marigold seeds have been exposed to, her mother, Beatrice, is decaying. As she does so she radiates an horrific energy. Embittered by her own failings, she seeks vengeance on everyone around her. Her eldest daughter, Ruth, is a pretty, outgoing girl who is subject to fits and has not achieved at school. Tillie, on the other hand, is plain and painfully shy but has a natural gift and enthusiasm for science. Beatrice seems incapable of giving her daughters the love they need and showing pride in them. Instead, she mocks and hurts them but at the same time clings to them and tries to stop them having a life of their own. Also living in the house is a decrepit old woman lodger referred to as Nanny. Beatrice treats the old lady with loathing, perhaps because Nanny seems to represent what she herself may become: ugly, unloved, abandoned.

The style of the play

The Effect of Gamma Rays on Man-in-the-Moon Marigolds is very much part of an American tradition of drama which requires actors to explore the characters in a special way. Many famous American actors such as Marlon Brando, Dustin Hoffman and Joanna Woodward (who played the part of Beatrice in the 1972 film version of the play) were trained in what is known as 'The Method', an intensive, deeply psychological approach to acting aimed at giving characters an emotional depth rather than having the actors playing the parts in a showy, theatrical way. The result of this style of acting helps make plays like this seem claustrophobic. The characters appear to be trapped by their environment; like caged rats they turn on each other rather than doing anything positive to escape. This is certainly true of Ruth and Beatrice. By contrast, Tillie seems to offer a ray of hope. Despite the bickering and decay she is faced with in her home life, she has been touched by the wonder and beauty of the universe outside and the possibility that things not only can, but inevitably will, change. Even though she only has a small voice, there is a great truth and power to her insight. The play won the Pulitzer Prize for Literature in 1971.

The extract

The Effect of Gamma Rays on Man-in-the-Moon Marigolds is quite a short play and this extract is an edited version of Act 2. In the first Act Ruth has been embarrassed by seeing Tillie on the school stage presenting a class assembly on a science topic. When Tillie gets to the final of the science competition, though, she feels genuinely proud of her achievement. Beatrice also seems proud of Tillie but doesn't know how to show it. It is the evening of the competition finals and the shy Tillie will have to present the findings of her experiment in public. When Beatrice tries to make Ruth stay at home to look after Nanny, Ruth cruelly tells her mother what the staff at the school have been saying about her. Beatrice is humiliated. She refuses to go to the presentation, gets drunk and wreaks a terrible revenge on all around her. In doing so, she hurts herself as much as anyone else.

RUTH   Miss Hanley was telling Mr Goodman about Mama . . . when
she found out you were one of the top five winners. And he wanted
to know if there was something wrong with Mama because she
sounded crazy over the phone. And Miss Hanley said she *was* crazy
and she always has been crazy and she can't wait to see what she   5
looks like after all these years. Miss Hanley said her nickname used
to be Betty the Loon.

TILLIE   [*as* RUTH *brushes her hair, brusquely*]   Ruth, you're hurting me.

RUTH   She was just like you and everybody thought she was a big
weirdo. There! You look much better! [*She goes to the rabbit cage.*] If   10
anybody stuck you in a pot of boiling water I'd kill them, do you
know that? [*To* TILLIE.] What do they call boiling the skin off a cat?
I call it murder, that's what I call it. They say it was hit by a car and
Janice just scooped it up and before you could say *bingo* it was
screaming in a pot of boiling water. Do you know what they're all   15
waiting to see? Mama's feathers! That's what Miss Hanley said. She
said Mama blabs as though she was the Queen of England and just
as proper as can be and that her idea of getting dressed up is to put
on all the feathers in the world and go as a bird. Always trying to
get somewhere like a great big bird.   20

TILLIE   [*rises*]   Don't tell Mama, please. It doesn't matter.

RUTH   I was up there watching her getting ready and sure enough
she's got the feathers out.

TILLIE   You didn't tell her what Miss Hanley said?

RUTH   Are you kidding? I just told her I really didn't like the feathers   25
and I didn't think she should wear any. But I'll bet she doesn't listen
to me.

TILLIE   It doesn't matter.

RUTH   It doesn't matter? Do you think I want to be laughed right out
of the school tonight with Chris Burns there and all? Laughed right   30
out of the school with your spaghetti hair and her feathers on that
stage, and Miss Hanley just splitting her sides.

TILLIE   Promise me you won't say anything.

RUTH   On one condition.

TILLIE   What?   35

RUTH   Give Peter to me.

TILLIE   [*pause*]   The taxi will be here any minute and I won't have all
this stuff ready. Did you see my speech?

RUTH   I mean it. Give Peter to me.

TILLIE   He belongs to all of us.   40

RUTH   For me. All for me. What do you care? He doesn't mean anything to you anymore now that you've got all those crazy plants.

TILLIE [RUTH *grabs* TILLIE's *arm*]   Will you stop?

RUTH   If you don't give him to me I'm going to tell Mama that every-   45
body's waiting to laugh at her.

TILLIE [*picks up the cage, looking for her speech*]   Where are those type-
written cards?

RUTH [*holding onto the cage with* TILLIE]   I MEAN IT! Give him to
me!

TILLIE   Does he mean that much to you?   50

RUTH   Yes!

TILLIE All right . . . [*Releases the cage to* RUTH *who takes out the rabbit.*]

RUTH [*she laughs*]   Betty the Loon . . . [*She laughs again.*] That's what
they used to call her, you know. Betty the Loon!

TILLIE   I don't think that's very nice.   55

RUTH   First they had Betty the Loon and now they've got Tillie the
Loon. [*To the rabbit.*] You don't have to worry about me turning you
in for any old plants. [*Pause.*] How much does a taxi cost from here
to the school?

TILLIE   Not much . . .   60

RUTH   I wish she'd given me the money it cost for a taxi and all that
cardboard and paint and flower pots and stuff. The only time she
ever made a fuss over me was when she drove me nuts.

TILLIE   Tell her to hurry, please.

RUTH   By the way, I went over to see Janice Vickery's pot that she did   65
you know what in and I started telling her and her mother about
the worms in Mr Alexander Brougham's legs and I got thrown out
because it was too near dinnertime. That Mrs Vickery kills me. She
can't stand worms in somebody else's legs but she lets her daughter
cook a cat.   70

TILLIE [*calling*]   Mother! The taxi will be here in a minute.

BEATRICE [*off up stairs*]   You're lucky I'm coming without all this
rushing me. [BEATRICE *comes to the top of the stairs. There is a hint of
feathers around her. She is wearing high heels, and a turban on her head.
She is smoking a cigarette. She is even a little attractive tonight, and   75
though her words say she is greatly annoyed with having to attend the
night's function, her tone and direction show she is proud.*]

TILLIE   Mama, you look beautiful.

BEATRICE   Don't put it on too thick. I said I'd go and I guess there's
no way to get out of it. Do you mind telling me how I'm supposed   80
to get up on the stage? Do they call my name or what? And where
are you going to be? If you ask me they should've sent all the parents
a mimeographed sheet of instructions. If this is supposed to be such
a great event why don't they do it right?

TILLIE   You just sit on the stage before it begins, with the other 85
parents.

BEATRICE   How long is this thing going to last? And listen, I don't care
even if you do win the whole damn thing I'm not making any
speech. I can hold my own anywhere but I hated that school when
I went there and I hate it now . . . and the only thing I'd have to say 90
is what a pack of stupid teachers and vicious children they have.
Imagine someone tearing the skin off a cat.

RUTH   She didn't tear it off. She boiled it off.

BEATRICE   You just told me upstairs that girl tore the skin off with an
orange knife . . . Do you know sometimes you exasperate me? If 95
you've got all the plants in that cardboard box I can manage the
folding thing. Do you know I've got a headache from doing all these
titles? And you probably don't even like them.

TILLIE   I like them very much.

BEATRICE   Look, if you don't want me to go tonight I don't have to. 100
You're about as enthusiastic as a dummy about this whole thing.

TILLIE   I'm sorry . . .

BEATRICE   And I refuse to let you get nervous. Put that bow back in
your hair.

RUTH   [rises]   I took it out. 105

BEATRICE   What did you do that for?

RUTH   Because it made her look crazy.

BEATRICE   How would you know what's crazy or not? If that sweater
of yours was any tighter it'd cut off the circulation in your chest. The
bow looks very nice in your hair. There's nothing wrong with look- 110
ing proper, Matilda, and if you don't have enough money to look
expensive and perfect, people like you for trying to look nice. [She
finishes fixing TILLIE's hair by putting the bow back.] You know, one day
maybe you will be pretty. You have some nice features, when that
hair perks up and you learn some tricks with make-up. [She looks at 115
the plants in the cardboard box.] I hope you didn't crowd the plants
too close together. Did you find your speech?

TILLIE   Yes, Mother . . .

BEATRICE   You know, Matilda, I was wondering about something.
Do you think you're really going to win, I mean not that you 120
won't be the best, but there's so much politics in school? Don't
laugh, but if there's anyone who's an expert on that, it's me, and
someday I'm going to write a book and blast that school to pieces.
If you're just a little bit different in this world they try to kill you
off. 125

RUTH   [putting the rabbit in its cage]   Tillie gave Peter to me.

BEATRICE   Oh? Then you inherited the rabbit droppings I found upstairs. What are you doing with your coat on?

RUTH   I'm going out to wait for the taxi.

BEATRICE   Oh, no, you're not. You start in on the rabbit droppings or   130
you won't get another cigarette if you scratch my back with an orange knife.

RUTH   I'm going down to the school with you.

BEATRICE   Oh, no, you're not! You're going to keep company with that corpse in there. If she wakes up and starts gagging just slip her a shot   135
of whiskey. [*Taxi horn.*] Quick! Grab the plants, Matilda – I'll get the big thing.

RUTH   I want to go! I promised Chris Burns I'd meet him.

BEATRICE   Can't you understand English?

RUTH   I've got to go!   140

BEATRICE   Shut up!

RUTH   I don't care. I'm going anyway.

BEATRICE [*grabs* RUTH *and pushes her*]   WHAT DID YOU SAY? HA!

TILLIE   MOTHER! [*Taxi horn. Pause.*]

BEATRICE   Hurry up with that box, Matilda, and tell him to stop blow-   145
ing that horn. HURRY UP! [*To* RUTH.] I don't know where you ever got the idea you were going tonight. Did you think nobody was going to hold down the fort? Now you know how I felt all those years you and everybody else was running out – because there was always me to watch over the fifty-dollar-a-week corpse. [RUTH   150
crosses to the stairs. BEATRICE *stops her.*] Where are you going? If there's one thing I demand it's respect. I don't ask for anything from you but respect.

RUTH [*turns to* BEATRICE]   Why are you ashamed of me?

BEATRICE   I've been seen with a lot worse than you. I don't even know   155
why I'm going tonight, do you know that? Do you think I give one goddamn about the whole thing? [*Pause.*] Do you really want to know why I'm going? Do you really want to know why this once somebody else has to look out for that dried prune for a few min-utes? Because this is the first time in my life I've felt just a little bit   160
proud over something. Isn't that silly? Somewhere in the back of this turtle-sized brain of mine I feel just a little proud! Jesus Christ! And you begrudge me even that, you little bastard. [*Taxi horn.*]

RUTH   Hurry up. They're waiting for you. They're *all* waiting for you.

BEATRICE [*picks up* TILLIE's *display board*]   I hope the paint is dry.   165
Who's waiting for me?

RUTH   Everybody . . . including Miss Hanley. She told all the teachers about you . . . and they're all waiting.

BEATRICE   You're such a little liar, Ruth, do you know that? When you
    can't have what you want you try to ruin it for everybody else.   170
RUTH   Good night, Betty the Loon. [BEATRICE *stops as if she's been
    stabbed. After a moment she drops the display board and then turns. Taxi
    horn.*]
BEATRICE [*she removes the turban. She throws the turban, purse and gloves
    down.*]   Put your coat on.   175
RUTH   What for?
BEATRICE   Take this thing and go with Matilda.
RUTH   I don't want to go now.
BEATRICE   GET OUT OF HERE!
RUTH [*pause*]   Now she's going to blame it on me you're not going –   180
    and take the rabbit back. [*Taxi horn.*] I can't help it what people call
    you. [*Pause.*] I'll tell Tillie you'll be down later, all right? [*Pause.*]
    Don't answer me. What do I care! [*She exits and slams the door.*
    BEATRICE *stands alone. She begins to sob quietly, and slowly starts to
    remove her dress as a music theme fades in and the lights fade out.*]   185

* * *

As the lights fade up, BEATRICE *enters. She is wearing a robe, open
down the front. She has obviously been drinking and she is carrying a
glass half full of whiskey. She picks up the phone book, finds the number, crosses to the phone, and dials.*

BEATRICE [*into the phone*]   I want to speak to the principal, please.
    [*Pause.*] Well, you'll just have to get him down off the stage. [*Pause.*]
    It's none of your goddamn business who I am! [*Pause.*] Oh, I see.
    [*Pause.*] Yes. I have a message for him and Mr Goodman, and for
    you too. And this is for Miss Hanley, too . . . Tell them Mrs   190
    Hunsdorfer called to thank them for making her wish she was dead
    . . . Would you give them that message, please? [*Pause.*] Thank you
    very much. [*She hands the phone up. Pause. She takes a drink from the
    glass. Telephone rings. She ignores it. Telephone stops ringing. She dials
    another number. Into the phone.*] This is Mrs Hunsdorfer. [*Pause.*] I'm   195
    sorry if I frightened you. I wouldn't want you to think that Nanny
    had deceased or anything like that – I can imagine how terrible
    you'd feel if anything like that ever happened . . . Terrible tragedy
    that would be, Miss Career Woman of the Year. [*Pause.*] Yes, I'll tell
    you why I'm calling. I want her out of here by tomorrow. I told you   200
    when you rolled her in here I was going to try her out for a while
    and if I didn't like her she was to get the hell out. Well, I don't like
    her so get her the hell out. [*Pause.*] It's like this. I don't like the way
    she cheats at solitaire. Is that a good enough reason? [*Pause.*] Fine.

And if she's not out of here by noon I'll send her collect in an ambu-   205
lance, you son of a bitch! [*She slams down the phone and laughs quietly. She gets her glass and drinks. She looks at the rabbit in its cage at her
feet. She kicks the cage, and then again with violence. Pause. She rises,
looks in a cardboard box, finds a towel, throws it over her shoulder,
crosses to the table, gets the chloroform, puts the bottle in the pocket of*   210
*her robe, crosses to the rabbit cage, and picks it up. Pause. She exits up
the stairs. The stage is black by the time she is at the top of the stairs.*]

* * *

The lights come up on the platform. TILLIE *is standing to the right of
her display. The display consists of a display board and three pots of
the various mutations of marigolds. She is very nervous, and refers to
the cards.*

TILLIE   *The Past:* The seeds were exposed to various degrees ... of
gamma rays from radiation sources in Oak Ridge. [*Pause.*] Mr
Goodman helped me pay for the seeds. [*Pause.*] Their growth was   215
plotted against ... time. [*The first gong rings. She crosses to the left of
the display.*] *The Present:* The seeds which received little radiation
have grown to plants which are normal in appearance. The seeds
which received moderate radiation gave rise to mutations such as
double blooms, giant stems, and variegated leaves. The seeds closest   220
to the gamma source were killed or yielded dwarf plants. [*Gong.*]
The Future: After radiation is better understood a day will come
when the power from exploding atoms will change the whole world
we know. [*With inspiration.*] Some of the mutations will be good ones
– wonderful things beyond our dreams – and I believe, I believe this   225
with all my heart, THE DAY WILL COME WHEN MANKIND
WILL THANK GOD FOR THE STRANGE AND BEAUTIFUL
ENERGY FROM THE ATOM. [*Distant applause is heard. The lights
fade to a single soft light on* TILLIE's *face. Distant electronic sounds are
heard. With a soft cry.*] Mama! [*Again with a soft cry.*] Mama! [*The*   230
light fades out.]

* * *

In the darkness we hear RUTH *from off stage, picking up* TILLIE's *last
word 'Mama'.*
The lights fade slowly up on the room. Nothing has changed.

RUTH [*from off stage*]   MAMA! [*She enters the front door at a gallop,
with the display board.*] MAMA! SHE WON! WHERE ARE YOU?
SHE WON! [TILLIE *enters with the cardboard box and trophy under her*

arm. To TILLIE.] Hurry up! Hurry up! Oh, my God, I can't believe it! 235
Mama! Come on down! Hurry. [*She takes the trophy.*] Give me that!
Mama! Wait till you see this. [BEATRICE *enters from up stairs. She has*
been drinking a great deal.] Mama! She won . . . Didn't you hear me?
Tillie won the whole thing! [*She puts the trophy on the table.*] Mama?
What's the matter with you? What did you rip the paper off the win- 240
dows for?

TILLIE   Mama?

RUTH   What's the matter with you? Can't you even answer? I SAID
SHE WON! ARE YOU DEAF?

BEATRICE [*turns and faces* RUTH]   Ruth, if you don't shut up I'm going 245
to have you put away.

RUTH   They ought to put you away, BETTY THE LOON!

BEATRICE [*pause*]   The rabbit's in your bedroom. I want you to bury it
in the morning. [*Pause.*]

RUTH   If you did anything . . . I'll kill you. [*She exits up stairs.*] 250

TILLIE   Mama?

BEATRICE [*softly*]   Yeh.

TILLIE   You didn't kill it, did you?

BEATRICE   Nanny goes tomorrow. First thing tomorrow. [*There is a*
moan from RUTH *up stairs.*] 255

TILLIE [*crossing to the bottom of the stairs*]   Ruth? Are you all right?
[RUTH *enters from up stairs. She is carrying the dead rabbit, wrapped in*
the blue towel. She comes slowly down the stairs. At the bottom of the
stairs, her eyes roll back and her body begins to tremble.]

TILLIE   Mama . . . I think she's going to go. [RUTH *drops the towel and* 260
rabbit on the floor at TILLIE's *feet, the trembling getting worse and worse.*
TILLIE *follows her, trying to stop the oncoming attack. Softly.*] Don't go
. . . don't go, Ruth . . . don't go . . . [TILLIE *holding onto* RUTH, *the*
trembling at its worst.] Mama! Help me!

BEATRICE   Get the wooden spoon! [*She takes* RUTH *from* TILLIE *and* 265
helps her onto the sofa. BEATRICE *holds* RUTH's *feet.* TILLIE *runs to the*
counter, gets a wooden spoon, crosses to the sofa, puts the spoon under
RUTH's *tongue and holds her shoulders down. Finally, the convulsion*
passes. The room is silent.]

TILLIE   Shall I call the doctor? [*No reply.*] Shall I call the doctor? 270

BEATRICE   No. She'll be all right.

TILLIE   I think I'd better call the doctor.

BEATRICE   I didn't ask you what you thought!

TILLIE [*silence as* TILLIE *checks on* RUTH, *then picks up the dead rabbit*
wrapped in the towel, and holds the body close to her]   I'd better bury 275
him in the back yard.

BEATRICE   Don't bury the towel.

TILLIE   I'll do it in the morning. [*She puts the rabbit down, sits on the arm of the sofa and comforts* RUTH. NANNY *enters slowly unaware, des-iccated, in some other land. She shuffles to the table.*]   280

BEATRICE   [*not looking to* TILLIE]   Matilda?

TILLIE   Yes, Mama?

BEATRICE   I hate the world, Matilda. Do you know that?

TILLIE   Yes, Mama.

BEATRICE   I hate the world. [*A music theme fades in, and the lights begin   285
to very slowly dim.*]

TILLIE'S VOICE [*recorded*]   THE CONCLUSION: My experiment has shown some of the strange effects radiation can produce . . . [*She rises and crosses to the sink.*] and how dangerous it can be if not handled correctly. Mr Goodman said I should tell in this conclusion   290
what my future plans are and how this experiment has helped me make them. [*She crosses from the kitchen table to the foot of the stairs.*] For one thing, the Effect of Gamma Rays On Man-In-The-Moon Marigolds has made me curious about the sun and the stars, for the universe itself must be like a world of great atoms – and I want to   295
know more about it. [*The room is dark now except for a light on* BEAT-RICE *and* NANNY *and* TILLIE.] But most important, I suppose . . . my experiment has made me feel important – [*The light on* BEATRICE *and* NANNY *begins to slowly fade.*] every atom in me, in everybody, has come from the sun – [*She slowly faces front.*] from places beyond our   300
dreams. The atoms of our hands, the atoms of our hearts . . . [*The stage is completely dark except for the light on* TILLIE. *The tape fades out.*]

TILLIE   Atom. Atom. What a beautiful word. [*The light fades to black.*]

CURTAIN

Understanding the text

1   Draw a triangle and write the name of each of the major characters at each point. In a box beside each name write a list of words you would use to describe that character. Now, along each of the lines connecting the character names, write a few notes about the relationship between the characters.

2   Pick out three lines for each of the characters which you think are completely typical of them.

3   Perhaps it seems difficult to have any sympathy for Beatrice given how badly she appears to treat her daughters and the old lodger Nanny, but are there any moments in the extract when an audience might just begin to feel a little sorry for her?

4   *The Effect of Gamma Rays on Man-in-the-Moon Marigolds* is an American play. Find five examples of language that indicate this; you may pick out individual words, or perhaps you can find whole phrases that have a distinctive American 'feel' to them.

5   What different types of status does each character possess? Draw three columns and put the name of each character at the top of each one. List the strengths of each character, that is, the things that give them some sort of power in the household; then jot down their weaknesses, that is, the things that make them vulnerable.

6   There are a number of aspects of this play which seem quite symbolic. For example, what Tillie discovers about the effect of gamma rays on man-in-the-moon marigolds could be taken as a parallel to what is happening in her family. What other examples of symbolism can you find in the extract and what do they suggest to you? Think about, for example, the rabbit, Nanny shuffling on at the end and Tillie's last line: 'Atom. Atom. What a beautiful word.'

Producing the scene

1   Apart from Tillie's presentation at the science competition the play is set in one room. Ruth and Beatrice are at each other's throats all the time, while Tillie patiently waits for something better from the world outside. Sketch a design for the set and make some suggestions for lighting the room that would emphasise how claustrophobic the atmosphere of the apartment is.

2   Beatrice, Ruth and Tillie are very different characters. How could their personalities be shown in the way they are costumed in this extract? Sketch and describe costume designs for at least two of the characters to illustrate their contrasting personalities.

3   This extract presents a number of very difficult challenges for actors (it's perhaps not surprising that Joanna Woodward won an Oscar for her performance as Beatrice in the film version). In groups of three, work on the moment when Ruth says 'Good night, Betty the Loon' and the effect it has on Beatrice. One of you should act as a director to help the two actors make the best use of positioning on stage and timing.

4   In pairs, work on either the scene in which the drunken Beatrice makes her telephone calls or Tillie's last speech. Again, one of you should act as a director to help the actor make their use of voice effective. Pay particular attention to the effect well-placed pauses can have.

5   Another particularly challenging instance to stage is when Ruth enters with the dead rabbit and starts to have a fit. In small groups, work on the section starting with Tillie's line 'Ruth? Are you all right?' to when Beatrice says 'Don't bury the towel'. Talk about how you would want an audience to feel about each of the characters in this section and rehearse it. Take your time and consider what extra 'stage-business' you might add to help achieve the audience response you want.

6   The stage direction just before Tillie's last speech suggests that music is used to add to the atmosphere. What sort of music would you choose to underscore the end of the play? Try to find a few possible pieces and talk about what would make the most suitable choice.

Further development

1   In pairs, improvise a scene in which one person (A) is behaving selfishly and insensitively while the other (B) tries patiently to get on with something important to them. A should look for opportunities to attract B's attention. Although B must remain calm in front of A, what could they do to show the audience that they are in fact getting increasingly frustrated with the situation?

2   In groups of three, imagine a scene in which Beatrice says that she intends to visit the school to complain about the way the staff there have been talking about her. How would Ruth and Tillie react to this? You might start your improvisation with Beatrice saying, 'I'm going straight down to that school and then they'll see just how crazy I am . . .'

3   Work in pairs to explore the character of Beatrice. Think about the way she presents herself 'in public' and what she might be thinking and feeling behind this. After some preparation, work as a whole class to hot-seat two volunteers in role as Beatrice. For each question asked there should be two answers, one from the 'public' Beatrice, and one from the 'private' one.

4   Consider the themes of decay and escape that are apparent in the play. In a small group, devise a sequence of movements that could suggest how one character finds a way of breaking out from a situation which is oppressive and destructive. If possible, you should try to find a piece of music that could be played as a background to your movement.

5   Why do you suppose Beatrice has become so bitter and twisted? Work in small groups to devise a scene from her past which might help explain why she is as she is. As a whole class, share these scenes one after the other as a collage of Beatrice's past life.

6   Imagine that Tillie grows up to be an eminent scientist and is invited to appear on a television chat show. In pairs, one of you should adopt the role of the interviewer while the other plays Tillie. The interviewer is particularly

interested in Tillie's childhood and home life. What do you think the adult Tillie might say about her mother and sister and how would she say it?

7 Both Tillie and Beatrice have monologues in this extract. If Ruth were to have the chance to speak directly to the audience what would she say? Write and rehearse a monologue for Ruth and decide at what point in the extract you might place it for the best effect on the way the audience felt about her as a character.

EXAMPLE

by the Belgrade TIE company

CAST (in order of appearance)

PETITIONER

PROCTER

PASSER-BY

NARRATOR

SPOKESMAN (OFFSTAGE)

MRS BENTLEY

SILVERMAN

SPEAKER

DEREK BENTLEY

9 speaking parts. Doubling possible.

TIE stands for Theatre in Education. A great many schools now enjoy visits from TIE teams – perhaps your school is one of them. The aim of these teams of actor/teachers is to use the theatre's ability to excite and involve young people to help them discover and understand something new.

Some TIE shows set up problems which require the audience to get actively involved in the finding of a solution. Others present a play which needs discussion and perhaps further research and practical work in order to understand the issues involved.

One such play is *Example*. It is the true story of Derek Bentley, who was hanged in 1953. Bentley had been involved in an attempted burglary with another boy, Christopher Craig, when they were apprehended by the police. Trapped on the roof of a warehouse, Craig shot dead a police officer. The penalty for murder at the time was death by hanging. However, Craig was only 16 years old and too young to hang. Bentley, on the other hand, was 19, and although he was clearly not the murderer himself, the law judged that being older he was equally responsible.

The case caused a public uproar, particularly in the light of evidence that suggested Bentley had limited intelligence and had, in fact, given himself up to the police before the shooting took place. Despite all this the judges felt it necessary to make an example of someone. The play looks into the reasons why they felt this way, but suggests strongly that hanging Bentley was not a satisfactory solution.

The style of the play

The play is presented in short, episodic scenes, starting with a look at the life and character of Derek Bentley. Time is telescoped so that the opening scenes cover a span of years, whereas the later ones trace the events in the last weeks and then, finally, the last hours of Bentley's life. This technique gives the play a growing sense of urgency which should be reflected in the way it is presented.

The characters are mostly real people, but nevertheless seem to represent certain viewpoints. A problem in staging the play is to make these firm views come across without stereotyping the characters into 'goodies' and 'baddies'.

The extract

The last few scenes of the play are presented here. Bentley has been sentenced and his appeal has been refused. The tension mounts as every effort is made to spare his life. This tension is enhanced theatrically by the shortness and sharpness of the scenes.

Scene six

> The PETITIONER *enters, holding copies of the petition. She talks to the audience.*

PETITIONER   I've got here a petition for the reprieve of Derek Bentley. I've got nearly 100,000 signatures and need more. Will you read the petition and if you agree with it, please sign.

> *She hands them out to the audience, then sees* PROCTER.

PETITIONER   Will you sign this, sir?

PROCTER   [*looking at a copy*]   Petition of the reprieve of Derek Bentley.   5
Very interesting. Having any success with it?

PETITIONER   Most people sign. I reckon we'll get over 100,000 signatures.

PROCTER   100,000 eh? Not bad. [*She continues with handing out.*] Er
excuse me – are all these people against hanging?   10

PETITIONER   No, not all.

25

PROCTER   Just against hanging Derek Bentley?

PETITIONER   That's right.

PROCTER   Just a moment. One more thing – when you get all these signatures you're going to take them to the Home Secretary I presume?   15

PETITIONER   Yes, of course. He's the only one who can pardon Bentley now. Excuse me.

The PASSER-BY *enters.*

Excuse me, sir, will you sign the petition for the reprieve of Derek Bentley?   20

PASSER-BY   Sorry, no.

He starts to move off.

PROCTER   Could you tell me why you haven't signed the petition?

PASSER-BY   Who are you?

PROCTER [*producing press card*]   Harry Procter, Sunday Pictorial.

PETITIONER [*to* PROCTER]   If you're not going to sign the petition can I have it back as there are people here who'll sign.   25

PROCTER   Look, love, I'm trying to conduct an interview here. Are you blind? [*To* PASSER-BY.] Sorry about that, sir. Now, could you tell me why you didn't sign the petition?

PASSER-BY   I think it's a lot of fuss over nothing. If everybody goes mad with petitions every time some young thug gets sentenced to death, how will our police be safe?   30

PROCTER   So you think it's not fair to the police?

PASSER-BY   Very strongly. Who's thinking about the poor widow of the policeman now? Who's making a fuss about her? £2.16 a week pension that's all she gets. That'd be worth getting up a petition about.   35

PETITIONER   I agree but –

PASSER-BY   The real question is, can we really ask the police to risk their lives on our behalf if they don't feel they're supported by everybody and specially protected if things go wrong. That's the main point. How do you think they'll feel if this Bentley boy gets off?   40

PETITIONER   But –

PASSER-BY [*to* PETITIONER]   I'm sorry but your petition's a complete waste of time.   45

He goes.

PETITIONER [*calling after him*]   But Mrs Miles herself thinks Bentley
should be reprieved.

PROCTER [*to audience*]   Oh, yeah, did you hear about that? Touching
little scene it was. Policeman's Widow Says Bentley Should Not
Hang. I mean, not quite page one but pretty strong for page two.   50

PETITIONER   Look, are you going to sign or not?

PROCTER [*handing it back*]   I don't think I'll bother. I mean the Press
should remain impartial after all. And I mean, you've got more than
enough signatures for the Home Secretary.

The PETITIONER *has collected in the petitions during this.*

PROCTER   Do you mind if I come along to take a picture of your hand-   55
ing in the petition?

PETITIONER   If you must.

Slide of MAXWELL-FYFE, *Home Secretary.*

NARRATOR   Sir David Maxwell-Fyfe, Home Secretary.

PETITIONER   We would like to present a petition on behalf of Derek
William Bentley at present under sentence of death.   60

A hand appears to receive the petition from her. PROCTER *takes photo.*

SPOKESMAN [*off*]   The Home Secretary will give your petition due
consideration. The parents of the prisoner will be informed of his
decision in due course. [*The* PETITIONER *tries to speak.*] That is all.

PROCTER   Thanks for the pic, mate. Don't reckon much to your
chances though.   65

PETITIONER   Oh really?

PROCTER   Yes, really. I mean Maxwell-Fyfe's not only the Home
Secretary, but he's also the head of the Police Force and it was a
policeman that got it wasn't it?

PETITIONER   Why don't you shut up, you parasite?   70

She goes. PROCTER *laughs.*

PROCTER   Well, we'll wait and see, won't we.

The slide of MAXWELL-FYFE *stays. The sound of heartbeats is heard.*
PROCTER *counts on his fingers, occasionally glancing at the slide of*
MAXWELL-FYFE.

PROCTER   Fifteen days to go
fourteen days to go
thirteen days to go
twelve days to go   75

eleven days to go
ten days to go
nine days to go
eight day to go
seven days to go   80
six days to go
five days to go
four days to go
three days to go
two days to go . . .   85

Scene seven

The slide and heartbeats fade. MRS BENTLEY *enters.* PROCTER *crosses to her.*

PROCTER   Mrs Bentley, Mrs Bentley, is it true the Home Secretary's rejected the petition?
MRS B   Rejected it?
PROCTER   You've heard nothing, Mrs Bentley?
MRS B   No, nothing. We're still waiting.   90
PROCTER   Oh.
MRS B   Why, what have you heard?
PROCTER   You've not had any word then?
MRS B   No messenger's been, nothing.
PROCTER   You've not had a letter, have you?   95
MRS B   Letter! . . . You'd better come in. The house is full of letters but surely . . .
PROCTER   Perhaps you'd better take a look through them, Mrs Bentley.
MRS B   But surely . . .   100
PROCTER   An official-looking envelope, Mrs Bentley, are you sure you haven't seen one?
MRS B   But surely they wouldn't send it by ordinary post. They couldn't leave us waiting.
PROCTER   Take a look, Mrs Bentley.   105

She brings out a large basket filled with letters. She empties it on the ground and starts searching through, eventually she finds the envelope. She opens it and starts to read.

PROCTER   Is that it, Mrs Bentley? What does it say?

She stays kneeling, silent and broken.

Look up, Mrs Bentley.

She looks up. He takes a photo. PROCTER *leaves. The heartbeats start up again. The mother stays on her knees.*

Scene eight

SILVERMAN [*as he enters*]   Mrs Bentley, Mrs Bentley –

Slide of SILVERMAN. *He goes to* MRS BENTLEY *and during the following, helps her up.*

SILVERMAN   My name's Silverman. I'm an MP. Some of us have heard about your son's case and want to do something about it.   110
MRS B   But the Home Secretary –
SILVERMAN   We're going to force a debate in the House of Commons tonight. There are important factors that weren't taken into account at the trial, factors such as your son's epilepsy and his low IQ. He must be reprieved. Will you come?   115

Pause.

MRS B   Yes, of course.

They cross the stage. Heartbeats again.

Scene nine

Sound of general hubbub. Slide: 'The Commons Debate 27th January 1953, evening.' SILVERMAN *shows* MRS BENTLEY *to a seat.*

SILVERMAN   Sit there, Mrs Bentley, in the public gallery.
SPEAKER [*tape*]   Order! Order!

Fade hubbub as SILVERMAN *starts.*

SILVERMAN   Mr Speaker! Mr Speaker, yesterday shortly after 7.00pm I presented for debate the motion 'that this House does not agree   120
with the Home Secretary's decision that there are not sufficient reasons for reprieving Derek Bentley, and urges him to reconsider the matter so far as to give effect to the recommendation of the jury and to the expressed view of the Lord Chief Justice that Bentley's guilt was less than that of his co-defendant, Christopher Craig.' I   125
have since been told by 'phone that on your instructions, the motion has been removed from the order paper. Is the House to wait until Bentley is dead before it is entitled to say he should not die?
SPEAKER [*tape*]   In this case the motion of the honourable member

which I saw last night dealt with the case of a capital sentence 130
which is still pending and there is a long line of authorities of all my
predecessors saying that, if a capital sentence is pending, the matter
shall not be discussed by the House.

SILVERMAN   Mr Speaker, this is a matter which arouses interest of the
deepest kind not merely in the House. I venture to think that if it 135
were possible to put such a matter to the vote today, there would be
an overwhelming majority of this House who think that the Home
Secretary has decided wrongly. I have here more than 200 telegrams
from all sorts of people all over the country, all of them except one
holding the decision to be wrong, and that one telling me to mind 140
my own business. Sir, I *am* minding my own business! That is why I
am raising this question with you. It is the business of all of us if this
boy is hanged when we think he ought not to be hanged. This is a
parliamentary democracy and we are all responsible for what occurs.

SPEAKER [*tape*]   A motion can be put down on this subject when the 145
sentence has been executed, the Minister responsible may be criticised on the relevant vote of Supply or on the Adjournment. I have
stated that this is the practice of the House and I cannot alter the
practice of the House.

SILVERMAN   A three-quarter witted boy is to be hanged for a murder 150
that he did not commit and which was committed fifteen minutes
after he was arrested. Can we be made to keep silent when a thing
as horrible and shocking as this is to happen?

SPEAKER [*tape*]   I repeat that no debate on the subject can be held
here until the execution has taken place. Only then can the justice 155
of that execution be debated. That is my ruling based on all available Parliamentary precedent.

> *Blank slide. Pause.* SILVERMAN *returns to where* MRS BENTLEY *sits*
> *silently.*

SILVERMAN   I'm sorry, Mrs Bentley.

MRS B   That's it then.

SILVERMAN   By no means, Mrs Bentley, don't give up now. A group of 160
us are going to go to the Home Secretary's house tonight to argue
with him face to face. We have signatures from 200 MPs. He must
listen to us. [*Pause.*] I think you should go to your son, Mrs Bentley.

> *Pause.*

MRS B   Yes.

SILVERMAN   We'll save him, Mrs Bentley. The Home Secretary will 165 listen. Go and see Derek.

Both leave. The heartbeats again. Silence.

Scene ten

Sound of crowd noises. PROCTER *dashes on and goes to the phone.*

PROCTER   The time 8.50am the 28th January, 1953, and only ten minutes to go before Derek Bentley is due to be executed. Outside
Wandsworth Prison a large and angry crowd has gathered to protest.
The chants of 'Murder . . . murder' changed to cheers a few minutes   170
ago when a telegram boy arrived but it was a false alarm. He was
not bringing Derek Bentley's reprieve. Even now extra squads of
police are standing by in case the crowd breaks into the prison to
try to save Bentley. With only minutes to go now, the crowd has
grown strangely quiet but no-one is leaving. The life of Derek   175
William Bentley now hangs on the thin thread of a last minute
change of heart by the Home Secretary who appears to have ignored
the deputation of MPs. Meanwhile, inside the prison, Derek
William Bentley dictates his last letter . . .

PROCTER *puts down the receiver and goes. Silence.*

Scene eleven

BENTLEY *enters.*

BENTLEY   Dear Mum and Dad, I was so glad to see you on my visit   180
today. I got the rosary and the letter and I saw the photo of the dog.
Iris looked nice surrounded by all those animals. I could not keep
the photo because it was a newspaper cutting. I told you, Mum, it
would be very difficult to write this letter. I can't think of anything
to say except you have all been wonderful the way you worked for   185
me. Don't forget what I told you, 'Always keep your chin up,' and
tell Pop not to grind his teeth. I hope Dad has more televisions in.
Oh, I forgot to ask him how things were on the visit. Oh, Dad, don't
let my cycle frames get rusty because they might come in handy one
day and, Dad, keep a strict eye on Denis if he does something   190
wrong, though I don't think he will, but you never know how little
things can get you into trouble. If he does, wallop him so that he
won't sit down for three weeks. I am trying to give you good advice
because of my experience. I tell you, Mum, the truth of this story
has got to come out one day and as I said in the visiting box, one   195
day a lot of people are going to get into trouble and I think you

31

know who those people are. What do you think, Mum? This letter may sound a little solemn but I am still keeping my chin up as I want all the family to do. Don't let anything happen to the dogs and cats and look after them as you always have. I hope Laurie and Iris get   200
married alright, I'd like to give them my blessing, it would be nice to have a brother-in-law like him. Laurie and I used to have some fun up at the pond till four o'clock in the morning, by the café. I always caught Laurie to pay for the pies, he never caught me. That will be all for now. I will sign this myself. Lots of love, Derek.   205

The heartbeats start up. BENTLEY *leaves. The heartbeats gradually fade. Pause. Enter* NARRATOR.

NARRATOR   Derek Bentley was hanged for the murder of PC Miles 28th January, 1953.

She leaves.

Understanding the text

1   One of the problems of any play, but perhaps TIE plays in particular, is to get information over to the audience so they can understand more clearly what is going on. Divide a sheet of paper into two columns and head them LINES and TECHNIQUES. Look at Scene Six and pick out all the lines and theatrical techniques that provide the audience with essential factual information. For instance, the Petitioner gets information across at the start of Scene Six by talking directly to the audience. Note the lines and techniques in the appropriate columns.

2   Procter appears in three of these scenes:
- What sort of person do you think the writers want us to think he is?
- Read through his lines again. What other special function does he appear to have?

3   Look at the last two scenes and read them aloud.
- What happens to the pace of the play here and how is this done?
- What effect does this have on the reader or audience?

4   What different viewpoints on the Bentley case are put forward in these last few scenes?
- Do you think the authors want you to think in a particular way about this case?
- Which arguments do you find particularly convincing?

Producing the scene

1   Note down the different locations for each scene. Devise a way of being able to move from one scene to another quickly so as not to break the mounting tension. Using spotlights on different areas would be one possible method, but if you use this technique you will need to consider appropriate colours, angles and intensities, and the spread of each area. Note down any other methods of dividing up the acting area which might be useful here.

2   *Example* may well be more effective if performed 'in the round', that is, with the audience sitting all around the acting area. What would be the advantages and problems of using such a technique for this extract?

3   List the sound effects specified in the extract. Discuss the effect of the heartbeats and having the voice of the Speaker on tape.

4   The stage directions suggest using slides at various places in the scene. What do you think the aim of this is and where could you position a screen on the stage to achieve this most effectively?

5   In performance *Example* tends to have a very emotional effect on an audience. One of the most touching moments is when Mrs Bentley finds the letter rejecting the petition and Procter tricks her into looking up so he can take a photograph of her crying. Rehearse this scene carefully and decide how best to change the pace in order to gain the most effect.

6   Read through the extract again, noting where and how tension is increased or lowered. Draw a graph to show how the pace of the extract varies. The horizontal axis should represent an approximate time scale (measured in key events and scenes) and the vertical axis should show the degree of tension and excitement. Label the points of highest tension which would excite an audience and also the 'troughs' where an audience is made to consider a line or effect more carefully.

Further development

1   A lot of the theatrical strength of *Example* comes from the way in which it changes the pace to capture and intensify emotional moments. Improvise a scene in which two or three people are enjoying themselves but then something happens which suddenly changes the atmosphere.

2   The Press are often criticised for the way they probe into personal tragedies in order to get their stories. Can you think of any incidents that have been reported recently where this may possibly have happened? Invent a story of your own in which a reporter seems to go too far in his/her attempt to get a 'scoop'.

3   *Example* raises some important and uncomfortable questions about why society sometimes feels the need to make an example of someone. Have you ever

been made an example of? Improvise a scene which shows someone being made an example of, but make it clear why those who are judging the person think it is the right thing to do.

4   *Example* could be described as a piece of 'documentary theatre', in that it uses a piece of history, and most of the characters in it really lived. The aim is to make an audience think about a real event and feel some of the emotions that the real characters must have felt. Simply hearing about events on the news or reading of them in the paper doesn't always give us a chance to understand the emotions experienced by those involved. Try to think of a real event, recent or past, that you feel deserves exploring in this way.

- In groups make a tableau depicting any scene from the incident
- Take it in turns to leave the tableau and imagine that you are a newspaper photographer. Focus on just one bit of the scene and invent a caption
- Discuss what effect your different photographs might have on an audience (if you have one you could actually use a Polaroid or digital camera for this exercise).

Imagine that just one of the pictures taken is shown in the papers. Improvise the scene in which one or all of the characters involved see it. What happens next?

INDIANS

by Arthur Kopit

CAST (in order of appearance)

SENATOR LOGAN

JOHN GRASS

SENATOR DAWES

SENATOR MORGAN

BUFFALO BILL

VOICE (OFFSTAGE)

*ANNIE OAKLEY

CHIEF JOSEPH

*INDIANS, ROUGHRIDERS AND ROUSTABOUTS

7 speaking parts. Doubling possible.
*Non-speaking parts.

Most of what people in Europe know about the North American Indian has probably come from films and television shows made in America by white Americans. Through the treatment they are given in the Hollywood Western, it is easy to view Indians as mindless savages who stood in the way of progress represented by brave settlers and pioneers plunging into the wilderness in their wagon trains. The fact that the wilderness is now prosperous ranch land seems to suggest that even though many were killed, the end result was worth it. It seems appropriate that the films that have given us so many ideas about the opening up of America were made in California – the end of the long trail west. When John Wayne made his films he perhaps saw his work as honouring his forefathers who had taken risks that made the nation great.

But there is another side to the story that is less palatable than the popular one seen in the cinema. Characters like Sitting Bull, Geronimo and Crazy Horse aren't just fictional. They were real men who, in one way or another, fought for what they saw as their birthright – free passage across a vast land. In the space of less than a century the age-old tribes of plains Indians were reduced from populous, thriving nations with their own traditions and histories, to small bands held in barren reservations. Many tribes were wiped out completely by starvation or massacre as they were gradually herded out of their homelands into the areas that the white man didn't want.

Buffalo Bill and Wild Bill Hickok were also real characters. Born William F. Cody, Buffalo Bill acquired his nickname after he slaughtered 4,280 buffaloes to feed the men building the railroad. Unfortunately not only did the men not like the meat, the buffalo reproduces so slowly that the kill seriously damaged the Indians' food supply for years afterwards. In 1883 Cody set up a 'Wild West Show' which used circus techniques and specially written playlets to depict the deeds of the frontiersmen. The great Sioux chief Sitting Bull was allowed to join the show and was, in fact, a friend of the affable Cody.

The style of the play

Indians is a complex piece of theatre which uses real people and real events but presents them in a very showy way in order to create a documentary about the destruction of the North American Indian and to make a critical comment on the trivial way in which history has been treated. Scenes depicting acts from Buffalo Bill's Wild West Show are intercut with scenes showing a meeting between US Government officials and Indians. It bears similarity to the play *Oh! What a Lovely War* which retells the story of the First World War largely through the use of popular song and comic sketches. The aim of both plays is to make the audience see history in a realistic rather than an idealised way. Like *Oh! What a Lovely War*, it is visually stunning to watch, and both funny and moving throughout.

The extract

Two scenes are presented here. In the first we see how the US Government can't understand the Indians' claims. The three senators try to keep their patience but basically see the Indians as stupid children. (They even tell the Indians that the President is 'The Great Father'.) However, the Indians' spokesman, John Grass, is anything but stupid and is able to hold his own in the battle of words. In sharp contrast to this intense situation, the second scene presents the audience with the glamour and fun of the Wild West Show. However, our sympathies are already turning to the Indians and we are moved and chilled by Chief Joseph's speech. The scene ends with an astonishing re-enactment of the Sundance which again contrasts the sham with the authentic.

Scene eight

Lights up again on the Senate Committee.

SENATOR LOGAN   Mister Grass. Let's leave aside the question of the steamboat. You mentioned the treaty at Fort Lyon and said that parts of that treaty had never been fulfilled. Well, I happen to be quite familiar with that particular treaty and happen to know that it is the Indians who did not fulfil its terms, not us.   5

JOHN GRASS   We did not *want* the cows you sent!

SENATOR LOGAN   You signed the treaty.

JOHN GRASS   We did not understand that we were to give up part of our reservation in exchange for these cows.

SENATOR DAWES   Why'd you think we were giving you twenty-five   10
thousand cows?

JOHN GRASS   We were hungry. We thought it was for food.

SENATOR LOGAN   It wasn't explained that *only* if you gave us part of your reservation would you receive these cows?

JOHN GRASS   Yes. That was explained.   15

SENATOR MORGAN   And yet, you thought it was a gift.

JOHN GRASS   Yes.

SENATOR LOGAN   In other words, you thought you could have both the cows and the land?

JOHN GRASS   Yes.   20

SENATOR DAWES   Even though it was explained that you couldn't.

JOHN GRASS   Yes.

SENATOR MORGAN   This is quite hard to follow.

SENATOR LOGAN   Mister Grass, tell me, which would you prefer, cows or land?   25

JOHN GRASS   We prefer them both.

SENATOR LOGAN   Well, what if you can't have them both?

JOHN GRASS   We prefer the land.

SENATOR LOGAN   Well then, if you knew you had to give up some land to get these cows, why did you sign the treaty?   30

JOHN GRASS   The white men made our heads dizzy, and the signing was an accident.

SENATOR LOGAN   An accident?

JOHN GRASS   They talked in a threatening way, and whenever we asked questions, shouted and said we were stupid. Suddenly, the   35
Indians around me rushed up and signed the paper. They were like men stumbling in the dark. I could not catch them.

SENATOR LOGAN   But you signed it, too.

Long pause.

SENATOR DAWES   Mister Grass. Tell me. Do the Indians really expect
    to keep all this land and yet do nothing toward supporting them-   40
    selves?

JOHN GRASS   We do not have to support ourselves. The Great Father
    promised to give us everything we ever needed; for that, we gave
    him the Black Hills.

SENATOR LOGAN   Mister Grass. Which do you prefer – to be self-   45
    sufficient or to be given things?

JOHN GRASS   We prefer them both.

SENATOR DAWES   Well, you can't *have* both!

BUFFALO BILL   *Please!*

JOHN GRASS   I only know what we were promised.   50

SENATOR DAWES   That's *not* what you were promised!

JOHN GRASS   We believe it is.

BUFFALO BILL   *What's going on here?*

SENATOR MORGAN   Mister Grass. Wouldn't you and your people like
    to live like the white man?   55

JOHN GRASS   We are happy like the Indian!

SENATOR LOGAN   He means, you wouldn't like to see your people
    made *greater*, let's say?

JOHN GRASS   That is not possible! The Cheyenne and Sioux are as
    great as people can be, already.   60

SENATOR MORGAN   Extraordinary, really.

BUFFALO BILL   Mister Grass. Surely . . . *Surely* . . . your people would
    like to *improve their condition!*

JOHN GRASS   We would like what is owed to us! If the white men want
    to give us more, that is fine also.   65

SENATOR LOGAN   Well, we'll see what we can do.

SENATOR MORGAN   Let's call the next. This is getting us nowhere.

JOHN GRASS   We would especially like the money the Great Father
    says he is holding for us!

SENATOR DAWES   I'm afraid that may be difficult, since, in the past,   70
    we've found that when an Indian's been given money, he's spent it
    all on liquor.

JOHN GRASS   When he's been given money, it's been so little there's
    been little else he could buy.

SENATOR MORGAN   Whatever, the Great Father does not like his   75
    Indian children getting drunk!

JOHN GRASS   Then tell the Great Father, who says he wishes us to live
    like white men, that when an Indian gets drunk, he is merely
    imitating the white men he's observed!

Laughter from the INDIANS. LOGAN *raps his gavel.*

SENATOR DAWES   STOP IT!   80

No effect. LOGAN *raps more.*

What in God's name do they think we're doing here? STOP IT!

Over the INDIANS' *noise, the noise of a Wild West Show is heard;*
lights fade to black.

Scene nine

Wild West Show music and crisscrossing multicoloured spotlights. The
rodeo ring rises from the stage, its lights glittering. Wild West Show
banners descend above the ring.

VOICE   And now, ladies and gentlemen, let's hear it for Buffalo Bill's
fantastic company of authentic western heroes . . . the fabulous
ROUGHRIDERS OF THE WORLD!

Enter, on heroically artificial horses, the ROUGHRIDERS *– themselves*
heroically oversized.
They gallop about the ring in majestic, intricate formation, whoopin'
and shootin' as they do.

With the ever-lovely . . . ANNIE OAKLEY!   85

ANNIE OAKLEY *performs some startling trick shots as the others ride*
in circles about her.

And now, once again, here he is – the star of our show, the Ol' Scout
himself; I mean the indestructible and ever-popular –

Drum roll

– BUFFALO BILL!

Enter, on horseback, BUFFALO BILL. *He is in his Wild West finery. He*
tours the ring in triumph while his ROUGHRIDERS *ride after him,*
finally exiting to leave him in the centre, alone.

BUFFALO BILL   THANK YOU, THANK YOU! A GREAT show lined
up tonight! With all-time favourite Johnny Baker, Texas Jack and his   90
twelve-string guitar, the Dancin' Cavanaughs, Sheriff Brad and the
Deadwood Mail Coach, Harry Philamee's Trained Prairie Dogs, the
Abilene County Girls' School Trick Roping and Lasso Society, Pecos
Pete and the –
VOICE   *Bill.*   95

BUFFALO BILL [*startled*]   Hm?
VOICE   Bring on the Indians.
BUFFALO BILL   What?
VOICE The *Indians*.
BUFFALO BILL   Ah.   100

> BUFFALO BILL *looks uneasily toward the wings as his company of* INDI-
> ANS *enters solemnly and in ceremonial warpaint; they carry the Sun
> Dance pole. At its summit is a buffalo skull.*

And now, while my fabulous company of authentic . . . American
Indians go through the ceremonial preparations of the Sun Dance,
which they will re-enact in all its death-defying goriness – let's give
a warm welcome back to a courageous warrior, the magnificent
Chief Joseph –   105

> *Some* COWBOY ROUSTABOUTS *set up an inverted tub; music for* CHIEF
> JOSEPH's *entrance.*

– who will recite this . . . celebrated speech. CHIEF JOSEPH!

> *Enter* CHIEF JOSEPH, *old and hardly able to walk.*

CHIEF JOSEPH   In the moon of the cherries blossoming, in the year of
our surrender, I, Chief Joseph, and what remained of my people, the
Nez Percés, were sent to a prison in Oklahoma, though General
Howard had promised we could return to Idaho, where we'd always   110
lived. In the moon of the leaves falling, still in the year of our surrender, William Cody came to see me. He was a nice man. With eyes
that seemed . . . frightened, I . . . don't know why. He told me I was
courageous and said he admired me. Then he explained all about
his Wild West Show, in which the great Sitting Bull appeared, and   115
said if I agreed to join, he would have me released from prison, and
see that my people received food. I asked what I could do, as I was
not a very good rider or marksman. And he looked away and said
'Just repeat, twice a day, three times on Sundays, what you said that
afternoon when our army caught you at the Canadian border, where   120
you'd been heading, and where you and your people would have all
been safe.' So I agreed. For the benefit of my people . . . And for the
next year, twice a day, three times on Sundays, said this to those
sitting around me in the dark, where I could see them, a light
shining so brightly in my eyes!   125

> *Pause.*

He climbs up on the tub.
Accompanied by exaggerated and inappropriate gestures.

'Tell General Howard I know his heart. I am tired of fighting. Our chiefs have been killed. Looking Glass is dead. The old men are all dead. It is cold and we have no blankets. The children are freezing. My people, some of them, have fled to the hills and have no food or warm clothing. No one knows where they are – perhaps frozen. I 130 want to have time to look for my children and see how many of them I can find. Maybe I shall find them among the dead. Hear me, my chiefs. I am tired. My heart is sick and sad. From where the sun now stands, I will fight no more forever . . .

He climbs down from the tub.

After which, the audience always applauded me. 135

Exit CHIEF JOSEPH. *Pause.*

BUFFALO BILL   The Sun Dance . . . was the one religious ceremony common to all the tribes of the plains. The Sioux, the Crow, the Blackfeet, the Kiowa, the Blood, the Cree, the Chippewa, the Arapaho, the Pawnee, the Cheyenne. It was *their* way of proving they were . . . Indians. 140

Pause.

The bravest would take the ends of long leather thongs and hook them through their chest muscles, then, pull till they'd ripped them out. The greater pain they could endure, the greater they felt the Spirits would favour them. Give them what they needed . . . Grant them . . . salvation. 145

Pause.

Since the Government has officially outlawed this ritual, we will merely imitate it.

Pause.

And no one . . . will be hurt.

He steps back.
The dance begins. The INDIANS *take the barbed ends of long leather thongs that dangle from the top of the Sun Dance pole and hook them through plainly visible chest harnesses. Then they pull back against the centre and dance about it, flailing their arms and moaning as if in great pain.*

Suddenly JOHN GRASS *enters. A* ROUSTABOUT *tries to stop him.*
The INDIANS *are astonished to see this intruder;* BUFFALO BILL *stunned.*
JOHN GRASS *pulls the* INDIANS *out of their harness, rips open his shirt, and sticks the barbs through his chest muscles. He chants and dances. The other* INDIANS, *realising what he's doing, blow on reed whistles, urge him on. Finally he collapses, blood pouring from his chest.*
The INDIANS *gather around him in awe.*
BUFFALO BILL *walks slowly toward* JOHN GRASS; *stares down at him.*
The INDIANS *remove the Sun Dance pole and trappings.*
BUFFALO BILL *crouches and cradles* JOHN GRASS *in his arms.*
As lights fade to black.

Understanding the text

1 The Indians and the Senators have very different perceptions of their situation. Pick out two things that John Grass says that show how they really don't understand each other's way of thinking.

2 Look at Buffalo Bill's lines in Scene Eight. In what ways does his attitude to the Indians seem to differ from the Senators'?

3 The Voice seems to have two separate functions in Scene Nine. First it introduces the Wild West Show as a sort of Master of Ceremonies. What do you think its other function is?

4 Chief Joseph's line, 'After which, the audience always applauded me' seems to have the power to move audiences. Look at both parts of the speech again carefully and discuss why this line is so effective. Compare Chief Joseph's life in the circus with how he reports the life of the tribe to General Howard.

5 Look at the way tension is created at the end of both scenes. What it the effect of the abrupt switch from the meeting to the show?

Producing the scene

1 One way of achieving quick scene changes, as in this extract, is to have a split-level stage. Draw a diagram of how you could use a two-level stage to give the audience a good view of both scenes. How much room will you need for each scene?

2 Design or describe two contrasting costumes needed for these scenes. Consider how you might go about researching such costumes if you were actually asked to make them as authentic as possible.

3   Look at the stage direction, *Enter, on heroically artificial horses, the* ROUGH-
RIDERS *– themselves heroically oversized.* Design either a suitably heroic hobby-
horse or explain in words or with diagrams how the Roughriders might be made
to appear 'oversized'.

4   How could lighting effects be used to contrast the two scenes? Describe what
colours and types of lights you might use and, if possible, design a specimen lighting plot and cue sheet for these scenes.

5   As a director, what advice would you give to the actor playing Chief Joseph?
What *exaggerated and inappropriate gestures* could be used and where? Work in
pairs, one taking the role of the director and the other the actor attempting to
put these ideas into practice.

6   In small groups imagine the Senators, and perhaps some cavalry soldiers, are
posing to have their photograph taken before meeting the Indians. Decide, by
acting this out, how they would position themselves for such a photograph.
Adapt their postures in order to achieve an appropriate tableau for when the
lights come up on Scene Eight. Discuss what the tableau says about the characters depicted.

7   The final scene in which John Grass performs the sundance has, no doubt,
kept many directors awake at night because it is so difficult technically. You may
have seen the film *A Man Called Horse* in which the ritual is acted out. Look
carefully at the stage directions and discuss ways of achieving the effect described
in them.

Further development

1   A major theme of the play is the problem of two viewpoints clashing head
on. Make a list of as many other situations as you can think of where this happens. Divide the list into three sections:

  * those which are purely personal, for example a disagreement with your
parents over something
  * those which are social or cultural, for example which day of the week
should be set aside for worship
  * those which seem to be both personal and social, for example a conscientious objector refusing to fight for his/her country.

2   John Grass is driven to performing the sundance in a desperate attempt to
draw attention to his people's situation. Look at the list you made in Question
1. Are there any situations there that you know, or can imagine, have led to such
desperate acts? In pairs choose one situation and improvise a scene in which
actor A is explaining to actor B how and why they intend to make a point. Actor
B should be sympathetic but nevertheless try to find reasons why such an act
would be the wrong thing to do.

3   Replay the scene above, swapping roles, but making actor B totally unsympathetic to the cause. Compare the two scenes in terms of dramatic potential. What effect would each option have on an audience?

4   Switching styles quickly in order to 'shock' an audience into thinking about the content of a play is an effective technique. In this extract the depressing reality of the negotiations is sharply contrasted with the flashy and trivial presentation of the Wild West Show. Select a situation from the list prepared in Question 1 and write or improvise two scenes which treat the conflict in contrasting ways. For example, you could compare a news documentary report about an incident with a situation comedy which makes fun of the situation, or even compare the actual events of an incident with how they might be reported on the news.

5   With the aid of the teacher, divide the class into two. Imagine that one half is a group of pioneers who have taken considerable risks and made many sacrifices in order to 'open up the West' and make a living there. The other half is an Indian group which has lived on the land for centuries and has never felt the need to change its way of life. Each group has been given the opportunity of making a TV documentary about:

- what the current problem is
- how the problem came about
- what they think might happen next.

Show the documentaries to the other group. What is their reaction:

- in their character as an Indian or a Pioneer?
- as a member of the class?

6   *Indians* is a play which arose from the author's despair and frustration at real events as he saw them. A great deal of the power of the play comes from the fact that the events and characters are real, even if the way they are presented uses theatrical techniques. You could undertake an extended project of your own in which you research more thoroughly into one of the situations noted in Question 1 and find a way of presenting 'fact' in a theatrical way. Where would you start your research? Who could you talk to? What actual incidents could be dramatised? What theatrical techniques could you apply to moments in real life in order to make your point about them more clear to an audience?

THE VISIT

by Friedrich Dürrenmatt

CAST (in order of appearance)

MAYOR

CLAIRE ZACHANASSIAN

DOCTOR

ILL

GYMNAST

BUTLER

SCHOOLMASTER

*TOBY and ROBY, two gum-chewing giants

KOBY and LOBY, two blind eunuchs

MRS ILL

10 speaking parts. *Non-speaking parts.

After the Second World War dramatists were faced with a mighty problem – how could they make sense of and comment on the horror and destruction that had taken place? In Germany in particular, the question was, how could drama help try to explain what had made seemingly ordinary, reasonable people turn against their neighbours and send millions of them to death in the concentration camps? In Germany itself Hitler had ensured that any playwright who did not conform to the 'logic' of Nazi policies was either forced to flee the country (like the great playwright Bertolt Brecht) or put to death (like Joseph Câpek). It would take outsiders such as the Swiss playwrights Max Frisch and Friedrich Dürrenmatt to revitalise the German theatre. They did this by creating parables, that is, imaginative stories that somehow mirrored real events. What had happened in Germany in the 1930s was so bizarre that perhaps the only way to explain it was to tell bizarre stories.

The Visit is just such a tale. It is set in a small fictitious town, called Guellen, that has fallen on hard times. The factories have closed and the important international trains that used to stop there now go thundering through. (In Swiss German the word 'güllen' actually means 'liquid manure'!) However, Guellen has a famous daughter, the multi-millionairess Claire Zachanassian. When she announces that she is to return to her home town after an absence of 45 years there is much excitement and the belief that she will make the place great again. On her arrival she promises to give the townsfolk all they need – but at a price. As a girl she became pregnant by one of the town's young men, Alfred Ill, who then denied responsibility. Now she offers everyone in the town a vast sum of money on the condition that they kill him.

The story of *The Visit* can certainly be taken as a parallel to what happened in Germany under Hitler. People were given the promise of greatness so long as they delivered to the authorities anyone that the authorities thought were responsible for the country's decline. But the play is also a comment on attitudes that still exist. It shows how we can become trapped by the pursuit of riches and leisure and led towards evil deeds.

The style of the play

Although *The Visit* has a powerful moral message, Dürrenmatt's play doesn't preach in a high-handed way. Rather, he shows what happens when ordinary people with believable human weaknesses are confronted by extraordinary characters. The result is a grotesquely comic situation. Everyday humdrum reality becomes surreal as the people of Guellen try to carry on treating Alfred Ill as they always have while all the time plotting to do him in. A useful key for understanding and performing the play is Brecht's advice that we should:

Examine carefully the behaviour of these people:

Find it surprising though not unusual

Inexplicable though normal

Incomprehensible though it is the rule.

In other words, the more strange a character appears, the more they should be played as if they are perfectly ordinary!

The extract

In this extract the town sets out to impress their important visitor. This involves the Mayor making the town and Claire Zachanassian's own past sound rather better than it really is. Claire, however, quickly tells the truth and produces witnesses to show how she was wronged by the townspeople and Alfred Ill in particular. She states clearly how she expects justice to be done. The Mayor instantly rejects her extreme idea, but the seed has already been sown . . .

MAYOR   May I escort you to your place?

He escorts CLAIRE ZACHANASSIAN *to her place at table, centre, introduces her to his wife.*

My wife.

CLAIRE ZACHANASSIAN *examines wife through lorgnette.*

CLAIRE ZACHANASSIAN   Annie Dummermut, top of our class.

MAYOR *introduces her to a second woman, as worn out and embittered as his wife.*

MAYOR   Mrs Ill.

CLAIRE ZACHANASSIAN   Matilda Blumhard. I can remember you lying   5
in wait for Alfred behind the shop door. You've grown very thin and
pale, my dear.

DOCTOR *hurries in, right; a squat, thick-set fifty-year-old; moustachioed, bristly black hair, scarred face, threadbare frock-coat.*

DOCTOR   Just managed to do it, in my old Mercedes.

MAYOR   Doctor Nuesslin, our physician.

CLAIRE ZACHANASSIAN *examines* DOCTOR *through lorgnette as he kisses her hand.*

CLAIRE ZACHANASSIAN   Interesting. Do you make out Death   10
Certificates?

DOCTOR [*taken off guard*]   Death Certificates?

CLAIRE ZACHANASSIAN   If someone should die?

DOCTOR   Of course, Madam. It's my duty. As decreed by the authorities.   15

CLAIRE ZACHANASSIAN   Next time, diagnose heart attack.

ILL [*laughs*]   Delicious, simply delicious.

CLAIRE ZACHANASSIAN *turns from* DOCTOR *to inspect* GYMNAST, *clad in shorts and vest.*

CLAIRE ZACHANASSIAN   Do another exercise.

GYMNAST *bends knees, flexes arms.*

Marvellous muscles. Ever used your strength for strangling?

GYMNAST [*stiffens in consternation at knees-bend position*]   For strang-   20
ling?

CLAIRE ZACHANASSIAN   Now just bend your arms back again, Mister
Gymnast, then forward into a press-up.

ILL [*laughs*]   Clara has such a golden sense of humour! I could die
   laughing at one of her jokes!   25

DOCTOR [*still disconcerted*]   I wonder. They chill me to the marrow.

ILL [*stage whisper*]   She's promised us hundreds of thousands.

MAYOR [*gasps*]   Hundreds of thousands?

ILL   Hundreds of thousands.

DOCTOR   God Almighty.   30

The millionairess turns away from GYMNAST.

CLAIRE ZACHANASSIAN   And now, Mister Mayor, I'm hungry.

MAYOR   We were just waiting for your husband, my dear lady.

CLAIRE ZACHANASSIAN   You needn't. He's fishing. And I'm getting a
   divorce.

MAYOR   A divorce?   35

CLAIRE ZACHANASSIAN   Moby'll be surprised too. I'm marrying a
   German film star.

MAYOR   But you told us it was a very happy marriage.

CLAIRE ZACHANASSIAN   All my marriages are happy. But when I was a
   child I used to dream of a wedding in Guellen Cathedral. You should   40
   always fulfil your childhood dreams. It'll be a grand ceremony.

All sit. CLAIRE ZACHANASSIAN *takes her place between* MAYOR *and*
ILL. ILL's *wife beside* ILL, MAYOR's *wife beside* MAYOR. SCHOOL-
MASTER, PRIEST *and* POLICEMAN *at separate table, right. The four
citizens, left. In background, more guests of honour, with wives.
Above, the banner: 'Welcome Clarie'.* MAYOR *stands beaming with
joy, serviette already in position, and taps on his glass.*

MAYOR   My dear lady, fellow-citizens. Forty-five years have flowed by
   since you left our little town, our town founded by Crown Prince
   Hasso the Noble, our town so pleasantly nestling between Konrad's
   Village Wood and Pückenried Valley. Forty-five years, more than four   45
   decades, it's a long time. Many things have happened since then,
   many bitter things. It has gone sadly with the world, gone sadly with
   us. And yet we have never, my dear lady – our Clarie [*Applause.*] –
   never forgotten you. Neither you, nor your family. Your mother, that
   magnificent and robustly healthy creature [ILL *whispers something to*   50
   him.] tragically and prematurely torn from our midst by tuberculosis,
   and your father, that popular figure, who built the building by the
   station which experts and laymen still visit so often [ILL *whispers*
   something to him.] – still admire so much, they both live on in our
   thoughts, for they were of our best and worthiest. And you too, my   55
   dear lady: who, as you gambolled through our streets – our streets,

alas, so sadly decrepit nowadays – you, a curly-headed, blonde [ILL *whispers something to him.*] – redheaded madcap, who did not know you? Even then, everyone could sense the magic in your personality, foresee your approaching rise to humanity's dizzy heights. [*Takes out his notebook.*] You were never forgotten. Literally never. Even now, the staff at school hold up your achievements as an example to others, and in nature studies – the most essential ones – they were astonishing, a revelation of your sympathy for every living creature, indeed for all things in need of protection. And even then, people far and wide were moved to wonder at your love of justice, at your sense of generosity. [*Huge applause.*] For did not our Clarie obtain food for an old widow, buying potatoes with that pocket-money so hardly earned from neighbours, and thereby save the old lady from dying of hunger, to mention but one of her deeds of charity. [*Huge applause.*] My dear lady, my dear Guelleners, that happy temperament has now developed from those seeds to an impressive flowering, and our red-headed madcap has become a lady whose generosity stirs the world; we need only think of her social work, of her maternity homes and her soup kitchens, of her art foundations and her children's nurseries, and now, therefore, I ask you to give three cheers for the prodigal returned: Hip, Hip, Hip, Hurrah! [*Applause.*]

CLAIRE ZACHANASSIAN *gets to her feet.*

CLAIRE ZACHANASSIAN   Mister Mayor, Guelleners. I am moved by your unselfish joy in my visit. As a matter of fact I was somewhat different from the child I seem to be in the Mayor's speech. When I went to school, I was thrashed. And I stole the potatoes for Widow Boll, aided by Ill; not to save the old bawd from dying of hunger, but just for once to sleep with Ill in a more comfortable bed than Konrad's Village Wood or Petersens' Barn. None the less, as my contribution to this joy of yours, I want to tell you I'm ready to give Guellen one million. Five hundred thousand for the town and five hundred thousand to be shared among each family.

Deathly silence.

MAYOR [*stammers*]   One million.

Everyone still dumbstruck.

CLAIRE ZACHANASSIAN   On one condition.

Everyone bursts into indescribable jubilation, dancing round, standing on chairs, GYMNAST *performing acrobatics, etc.* ILL *pounds his chest enthusiastically.*

ILL There's Clara for you! What a jewel! She takes your breath away! Just like her, O my little sorceress! 90

 Kisses her.

MAYOR Madam: you said, on one condition. May I ask, on what condition?

CLAIRE ZACHANASSIAN I'll tell you on what condition. I'm giving you a million, and I'm buying myself justice.

 Deathly silence. 95

MAYOR My dear lady, what do you mean by that?
CLAIRE ZACHANASSIAN What I said.
MAYOR Justice can't be bought.
CLAIRE ZACHANASSIAN Everything can be bought.
MAYOR I still don't understand.
CLAIRE ZACHANASSIAN Boby. Step forward. 100

 BUTLER *steps forward, from right to centre, between the three tables. Takes off his dark glasses.*

BUTLER I don't know if any of you here still recognise me.
SCHOOLMASTER Chief Justice Courtly.
BUTLER Right. Chief Justice Courtly. Forty-five years ago, I was Lord Chief Justice in Guellen. I was later called to the Kaffigen Court of Appeal until, twenty-five years ago it is now, Madam Zachanassian 105 offered me the post of Butler in her service. A somewhat unusual career, indeed, I grant you, for an academic man, however, the salary involved was really quite fantastic . . .
CLAIRE ZACHANASSIAN Get to the point, Boby.
BUTLER As you may have gathered, Madame Claire Zachanassian is 110 offering you the sum of one million pounds, in return for which she insists that justice be done. On other words, Madame Zachanassian will give you all a million if you right the wrong she was done in Guellen. Mr Ill, if you please.

 ILL *stands. He is pale, startled, wondering.* 115

ILL What do you want of me?
BUTLER Step forward, Mr Ill.
ILL Sure.

 Steps forward, to front of table, right. Laughs uneasily. Shrugs.

BUTLER The year was nineteen ten. I was Lord Chief Justice in Guellen. I had a paternity claim to arbitrate. Claire Zachanassian, at the time Clara Wascher, claimed that you, Mr Ill, were her child's father. 120

ILL *keeps quiet.*

At that time, Mr Ill, you denied paternity. You called two witnesses.
ILL   Oh, it's an old story. I was young, thoughtless.
CLAIRE ZACHANASSIAN   Toby and Roby, bring in Koby and Loby.

The two gum-chewing giants lead pair of blind eunuchs on to centre of stage, blind pair gaily holding hands.

BLIND PAIR   We're on the spot, we're on the spot!   125
BUTLER   Do you recognise these two, Mr Ill?

ILL *keeps quiet.*

BLIND PAIR   We're Koby and Loby, we're Koby and Loby.
ILL   I don't know them.
BLIND PAIR   We've changed a lot, we've changed a lot!
BUTLER   Say your names.   130
FIRST BLIND MAN   Jacob Chicken, Jacob Chicken.
SECOND BLIND MAN   Louis Perch, Louis Perch.
BUTLER   Now, Mr Ill.
ILL   I know nothing about them.
BUTLER   Jacob Chicken and Louis Perch, do you know Mr Ill?   135
BLIND PAIR   We're blind, we're blind.
BUTLER   Do you know him by his voice?
BLIND PAIR   By his voice, by his voice.
BUTLER   In nineteen ten, I was Judge and you the witnesses. Louis
   Perch and Jacob Chicken, what did you swear on oath to the Court   140
   of Guellen?
BLIND PAIR   We'd slept with Clara, we'd slept with Clara.
BUTLER   You swore it on oath, before me. Before the Court. Before
   God. Was it the truth?
BLIND PAIR   We swore a false oath, we swore a false oath.   145
BUTLER   Why, Jacob Chicken and Louis Perch?
BLIND PAIR   Ill bribed us, Ill bribed us.
BUTLER   With what did he bribe you?
BLIND PAIR   With a pint of brandy, with a pint of brandy.
CLAIRE ZACHANASSIAN   And now tell them what I did with you, Koby   150
   and Loby.
BUTLER   Tell them.
BLIND PAIR   The lady tracked us down, the lady tracked us down.
BUTLER   Correct. Claire Zachanassian tracked you down. To the ends
   of the earth. Jacob Chicken had emigrated to Canada and Louis   155
   Perch to Australia. But she tracked you down. And then what did
   she do with you?

BLIND PAIR   She gave us to Toby and Roby, she gave us to Toby and Roby.

BUTLER   And what did Toby and Roby do to you?   160

BLIND PAIR   Castrated and blinded us, castrated and blinded us.

BUTLER   And there you have the full story. One Judge, one accused, two false witnesses: a miscarriage of justice in the year nineteen ten. Isn't that so, plaintiff?

CLAIRE ZACHANASSIAN [*stands*]   That is so.   165

ILL [*stamping on floor*]   It's over and done with, dead and buried! It's an old, crazy story.

BUTLER   What happened to the child, plaintiff?

CLAIRE ZACHANASSIAN [*gently*]   It lived one year.

BUTLER   What happened to you?   170

CLAIRE ZACHANASSIAN   I became a prostitute.

BUTLER   What made you one?

CLAIRE ZACHANASSIAN   The judgement of that court made me one.

BUTLER   And now you desire justice, Claire Zachanassian?

CLAIRE ZACHANASSIAN   I can afford it. A million for Guellen if some-   175
one kills Alfred Ill.

Deathly silence. MRS ILL *rushes to* ILL, *flings her arms round him.*

MRS ILL   Freddy!

ILL   My little sorceress! You can't ask that! It was long ago. Life went on.

CLAIRE ZACHANASSIAN   Life went on, and I've forgotten nothing, Ill.   180
Neither Konrad's Village Wood, not Petersens' Barn; neither Widow Boll's bedroom, nor your treachery. And now we're old, the pair of us. You decrepit, and me cut to bits by the surgeons' knives. And now I want accounts between us settled. You chose your life, but you forced me into mine. A moment ago you wanted time turned back,   185
in that wood so full of the past, where we spent our young years. Well I'm turning it back now, and I want justice. Justice for a million.

MAYOR *stands, pale, dignified.*

MAYOR   Madam Zachanassian: you forget, this is Europe. You forget, we are not savages. In the name of all citizens of Guellen, I reject your offer; and I reject it in the name of humanity. We would rather   190
have poverty than blood on our hands.

Huge applause.

CLAIRE ZACHANASSIAN   I'll wait.

Understanding the text

1 Pick out at least three moments in this extract which strongly suggest that *The Visit* is not a 'naturalistic' play but one that is more like a fairy tale.

2 Find out what terms such as 'parable', 'fable' and 'cautionary tale' mean. The story of *The Visit* clearly has a very strong 'moral'. From what you have read in this short extract, what do you suppose the moral of the story to be?

3 Dürrenmatt introduces many of the characters in *The Visit* as 'types' rather than giving them their own names. For example, in this extract we hear from the Mayor and the Doctor, while the Schoolmaster, Priest and Policeman are also present at the banquet. Pick out three things that these characters say or do which suggests that they are stereotypes. What do these stereotypes suggest about the nature of the people of Guellen?

4 The idea that drives the drama of *The Visit* is very straightforward and can be seen in many other plays and films. Basically, it involves establishing a sense of one sort of community, then introducing a character or event that will cause the community to question its own values. Can you think of any films or television dramas that work on the same idea?

5 At the end of this extract, the Mayor tells Claire Zachanassian that 'you forget, this is Europe. You forget, we are not savages'. Bearing in mind that the play was first produced just after the horror of the Second World War, such a line seems ironic. Can you think of things that have happened in Europe since that time which would suggest that the play's message is as relevant today as it was then?

Producing the scene

1 While the people of Guellen have fallen on hard times, Claire Zachanassian is not only fabulously wealthy but she has surrounded herself with an odd assortment of interesting characters, such as her mobster bodyguards Toby and Roby and the blind eunuchs Koby and Loby. Sketch and describe the costumes for at least two characters which would illustrate the difference between the dullness of the people of Guellen and the strangeness of Claire's entourage.

2 In groups, rehearse the section when Claire Zachanassian makes her offer. Start from her line, 'I'm ready to give Guellen one million' and finish with the Mayor's question, 'My dear lady, what do you mean by that?' You will need to think very carefully about how the actors should use their voices, facial expressions, gestures and position on stage to show that the atmosphere of the banquet changes at this moment.

3 In groups, or perhaps as a whole class, make a tableau of the scene at the point when Claire Zachanassian says, 'I'll wait.' What effect should this moment have on an audience? It would be useful to experiment with ways of showing·

- That different characters present have different attitudes towards her offer
- That while all those present may outwardly show disgust at her offer, inside they are all thinking the same thing!

4   In pairs, rehearse the Mayor's speech. On the surface, of course, he is trying to be complimentary and sincere, but one of you should act as director to help the other find ways of showing that he doesn't really know or understand anything about Claire Zachanassian at all.

5   Koby and Loby, the two blind eunuchs, are very odd characters indeed. To gain the best dramatic effect they need to be presented as rather funny, but underlying this there needs to be something rather chilling about them. In pairs, experiment with ways of saying their lines and moving as if they are one person that has been spilt into two bodies. Your aim in rehearsing this is to create an effect which would be intriguing but unsettling for the audience.

Further development

1   The dramatic interest of *The Visit* comes from the introduction of a character who is able to change the atmosphere and situation. With the help of the class teacher, form a large circle. One person will need to volunteer to start a simple action in the middle of the circle: cleaning a window, rowing a boat, taking the dog for a walk, for example. After just a few seconds the teacher will call 'FREEZE' and point to another member of the group who must then jump into the circle and somehow change the situation. So, for example, a person who was cleaning a window may be 're-activated' by the new character asking, 'Why are you picking those apples off my tree?' After a few moments of this new scene, the teacher will call 'FREEZE' again, at which point a third player will 'tag' the first one and start yet a new scene. This exercise relies on the players watching the actors carefully and thinking quickly. You may have worked like this before but, in this instance, each new player should try to change the tone of the improvisation. So, for example, if a pair of your classmates have created a comical scene, you need to think of a way of turning it into something strange, tragic or tense.

2   Before the arrival of Claire Zachanassian, Guellen is an incredibly boring town. How would people spend their time there? Watching the trains go past, perhaps? Reminiscing about times gone by? Devise a short scene that would impress upon an audience how dull life in Guellen had become.

3   The Mayor tries to make Claire Zachanassian's childhood sound rather better than it actually was. One of the ways in which he does this is to use *euphemisms*, that is, saying something in a very deliberately 'polite' way. For example, he

describes Claire's mother as a 'magnificent and robustly healthy creature' when what he might actually mean is that she an was overweight and scarily powerful woman! In pairs or small groups, improvise a scene in which a headteacher, perhaps along with a number of school governors, are trying to impress an important visitor by attempting to make things sound better than they obviously are. You might start your improvisation with a line such as, 'And here we have the drama room, which, as you can see, is full of joyous young souls experimenting with creative new ways of expressing themselves!'

4   Imagine that, thirty years from now, you are invited to speak at a school reunion. Decide whether you would say exactly what you feel about the place or whether you would prefer to disguise your true feelings behind a number of euphemisms. Write or improvise your speech.

5   In this extract, Claire Zachanassian offers the people of Guellen a stark moral choice: kill Alfred Ill and become rich, or keep him as your neighbour and stay poor. Such dilemmas are certainly dramatic in that they leave the audience wondering what they would do in such a situation. In small groups, devise your own scene in which someone is put into a position where they have to make a hard moral decision.

6   Alfred Ill is a shopkeeper whose business has not been doing well because nobody in the town has any money. Now that there is the possibility of every citizen becoming rich, how do you suppose the people of Guellen treat him once they have heard Claire Zachanassian's offer? In groups, improvise what happens in Alfred's shop the morning after the banquet. Do his customers feel sorry for him? Or do they try to buy things on credit in the expectation that someone, sometime, will give Claire Zachanassian the justice she demands?

7   Imagine that, at the end of the play, Alfred Ill does indeed die (to find out whether or not this actually happens you'll have to read or see the whole play, of course!). In groups, make a tableau that represents his funeral. How would people stand around his grave? Where would you place key characters such as his wife, the Mayor and Claire Zachanassian? If the audience could hear what different characters were thinking at the moment his coffin was lowered into the ground, what would they hear?

SHE'S DEAD

by *Paul Abelman*

CAST (in order of appearance)

1

2

2 speaking parts. No doubling.

She's Dead is one of the short plays published in a book called *Tests*. It was first published in 1966 and reflects the way people involved with the theatre at that time were putting a great deal of energy into exploring new forms and ideas.

Until the middle of the 1950s British theatre-going audiences were used to seeing plays which followed very conventional patterns. They were usually set in middle-class homes and were about middle-class people's problems. Sometimes they were referred to as 'well-made plays' which suggests that they were constructed in a careful but rather predictable way. However, a number of new ideas began to influence the British theatre. John Osborne's play *Look Back in Anger* is often seen as a play that shifted attention away from the middle classes and opened the way for the exploration of broader issues and viewpoints. In the East End of London, a director called Joan Littlewood was successfully staging the work of new young writers, and the strange 'absurd' theatre of Samuel Beckett was starting to appear in theatre clubs. The Royal Shakespeare Company had a young and revolutionary director called Peter Brook who, in the early 1960s, presented a season of plays under the title of 'The Theatre of Cruelty'. It must have been very exciting to see the theatre changing from being a place which provided entertainment for a select group of people into a place where new ideas could be developed and the assumptions and attitudes of the audience challenged.

The style of the play

She's Dead seems to extract humour from a very serious incident. Modern audiences or readers might see in it something of the style of *Monty Python's Flying*

Circus. This isn't surprising because the Python team were influenced by many of the things that were happening in the theatre at this time. However, the play is perhaps more than just a piece of daft humour – the last line, in particular, suggests that the author had deeper themes in mind when he wrote it.

Because it is a 'test', it is impossible to say how the play should be acted out or what the characters should be like. It is a piece of unfinished theatre which demands that the actors and director decide what they want to do with it and add their own creative and imaginative abilities to the performance.

1	By jove, you've murdered that woman!	
2	It's dreadful!	
1	Why did you do it?	
2	She provoked me. This is terrible.	
1	You've killed her. You've taken a human life!	5
2	It's appalling! This is the most frightful thing that ever happened to me.	
1	What have you done, man?	
2	I think I've killed this woman.	
1	Jove, how ghastly!	10
2	This is horrible. Yesterday – a year ago – how could I have dreamt . . .	
1	Look here, what have you done?	
2	My God, she's dead!	
1	How awful!	15
2	This is terrible.	
1	Well, there's one fortunate thing.	
2	Is there some consolation?	
1	There's one very happy aspect.	
2	Do you detect some glint of hope?	20
1	I'm a policeman. I can arrest you and make sure you pay the full penalty for your crime.	
2	I say, that is lucky.	
1	Strange that I should happen past, just after you'd done this dreadful thing.	25
2	It's most miraculous, isn't it? Things are never quite as bad as they seem at first glance.	
1	I'll see that you suffer.	
2	I feel I can depend on you.	
1	You'll sweat torments in a reeking prison, I'll ensure that.	30
2	It's very good of you.	

1 By jove, what's happened here?
2 I've killed this woman.
1 What have you done?
2 I've taken a human life. I've broken the sternest law of God and   35
   man.
1 Thank God, I'm a policeman.
2 Thank God for that!
1 Anguish is your portion from now on, until we take *your* life in
   some disgusting way.   40
2 How will you do it?
1 We'll probably strangle you with a length of rope. Nightmares are
   mere diversion compared to what's waiting for you.
2 It's lucky you passed by.
1 My God, man, what have you done?   45
2 Constable, I – I murdered this woman.
1 Why did you do it?
2 She picked a flower.
1 Provocation is no excuse.
2 She was my mother.   50
1 You've killed your mother. Matricide, you'll squirm! Your brain will
   buzz with horror until you crave the noose as a benefaction.
2 I loved this girl. She was a typist.
1 You've destroyed a typist, a useful citizen. Think of the letters that
   will blossom no more beneath her nimble fingers.   55
2 This woman was a barmaid.
1 The handle of the beer-pump will ne're more feel her touch.
2 What have I done?
1 You've taken a human life. Now, the facts: How did you kill her?
2 With my penknife! Officer, officer, it was unpremeditated. I merely 60
   took out my knife to admire the silver blade and then I felt I should
   try it out. So I stabbed Lilly twenty-four times.
1 Look at her blood, her innocent blood!
2 I stabbed her twenty-four times.
1 See, her blood's come out. That'll teach you to play with   65
   penknives.
2 Her blood – I didn't think it would all come out.
1 She was a blithe girl, a healthy thing – tell me what she was?
2 A song!
1 Yes, she was a song, a healthy thing. What was this girl?   70
2 Light.
1 Of course, she was light – she was the air, the breeze, the ripple in
   the air, but there was blood inside her.

2	I pierced her veins.	
1	What have you done?	75
2	Officer, I have a confession to make.	
1	Oh yes, sir?	
2	Yes, you see I seem to have – inadvertently of course – slain this girl.	
1	I see, sir. You realise, sir, that I shall have to report this?	80
2	Is that absolutely necessary, officer?	
1	It's the regulations, sir. I know that we often seem unnecessarily meticulous to the public but we have to register all misdemeanours.	
2	I say, I hope this doesn't mean I shall have to appear in court?	85
1	Oh no, sir. I shouldn't think anything like that. We get dozens of these little incidents.	
2	She was called Lilly, I think. You may want that for your records.	
1	Why did you kill her, sir? I might as well take all the facts.	
2	Why. Oh, I don't know. How can one assess every fleeting impulse? I met her in a pub, brought her out here to this remote spot, assaulted her –	90
1	Carnally?	
2	Yes, you know, rape and then I thought I might as well kill her as anything else.	
		95
1	Right you are, sir, I've got that. Perhaps you'd give me your name and address, sir? Just for our files?	
2	Is that really necessary?	
1	Well I would be grateful, sir. My sergeant's a stickler for detail.	
2	Very well, my name is Bill.	100
1	Bill, sir?	
2	Bombay Bill, also know as The Slaughterer.	
1	And your address, sir?	
2	Skull Lane.	
1	I say, what have you done?	105
2	Has something been done?	
1	There's a dead girl here.	
2	Did I do that?	
1	Have you killed this human being?	
2	Have I deprived someone of life?	110
1	At your feet, man, a dead girl!	
2	A girl you say? One wanting life?	
1	Why did you do it?	
2	You imply that there's some way of knowing why things are done?	
1	There's a gun here.	115

2   I fancy it's a revolver.
1   Is this your gun?
2   I have seen that weapon before.
1   Was this the cause of death?
2   A bullet leapt from its mouth.   120
1   This finger, this index finger on your hand – did it squeeze the
    weapon's trigger?
2   Pressure, generated by the muscles of my body, authorised by the
    synapses of my singing nerves, moved that little lever. The gun spat
    metal, a gob of metal which parted her soft tissues. I think it was   125
    then she died.
1   Have you slain this woman?
2   I? I have slain no-one. It was the gunmaker.
1   You killed this girl!
2   It was not I! It was a Hebrew who made the law she broke.   130
1   Then I must arrest you.
2   And are you really authorised to put a stop to history?
1   Jove, what have you done?
2   What I was told to do by the roots groping in the earth.
1   You've killed this girl.   135
2   By the numb stones nesting on the plain.
1   You'll pay for this.
2   By my accomplice the rain and his wild pal the wind.
1   To the cells!
2   Yes, come, brother, to the cells but first – wipe the blood from your 140
    hands too.

Understanding the text

1   There are several instances when comedy is achieved by someone making a
remark that doesn't seem to match the seriousness of the situation, for example,
'See, her blood's come out, that'll teach you to play with penknives.' Find at least
three other lines that create humour in this way.

2   The play suggests that you can view the same incident in totally different
ways depending on how and where you are. List the different reactions to the
murder shown in the play.

3   The play is full of contradictions. For example, the girl is described as the
murderer's mother, a typist and a barmaid. Things just don't appear to make
sense! Look through the play again and note the contradictions about who the

girl is and how she died. What do you think is being suggested by giving her so many identities?

4   The language of *She's Dead* has a strange and sometimes poetic quality to it. Things are described in unexpected ways; for example, the girl is described as being 'a song'. Pick out at least three lines which strike you as being 'poetic' or unusual in their use of language.

5   Look carefully at the last line. The murderer calls the 'policeman' his 'brother' and then tells him to wipe the blood from his own hands. Do you think these characters really are a murderer and a policeman or might they be representing somebody or something else? Are there any other lines in the play that suggest we are all somehow responsible for what happens to people?

Producing the scene

1   Given that the author makes no suggestions for the set or costumes, where would you set the play and how would you costume 1 and 2? Your suggestions here should depend on your conclusions in the last question.

2   Discuss various ways of staging the play; for example, as piece of theatre in the round; as a 'promenade performance' that might take place in the theatre foyer or even somewhere where people don't expect to see theatre at all; or on a conventional stage. What would be the advantages and disadvantages of these various ways of staging the play?

3   How important do you think it is actually to have a body on the stage? What would be the advantages and disadvantages of actually having it there?

4   Go through the script again and make a mark every time you think the characters are changing their attitude. If the whole play was acted with 1 and 2 keeping the same character throughout, it might be rather tedious to listen to and watch. Choose one of the changes you have identified and rehearse the few lines before and the few after, freezing at the precise moment when the change takes place. As you 'reactivate' from the freeze, adopt a completely different tone and type of voice and change your position and way of moving accordingly.

5   Using the same short section of the play, experiment with playing it at different speeds. Try delivering it in a fast, obviously comical way and compare this with a slow, heavy and menacing delivery. Are there places in the play where a change of pace might be effective?

6   Developing from Question 4, suggest a number of different character stereotypes that 1 and 2 could adopt in different places. (It might be worth looking at *The Body*, which also explores this technique.) For example, 2 could be a smooth business type when he says, 'Is that absolutely necessary, officer?' Choose another short extract and rehearse it in pairs using these stereotypes. What effects can

you achieve by using an obvious or unexpected characterisation in lines like 'My name is Bill . . . Bombay Bill, also know as The Slaughterer.'

7   Look again at the passage beginning 'Why did you kill her, sir? I might as well take all the facts' and ending 'I might as well kill her as anything else'. What is your immediate reaction to these lines? Is the author just making a sick joke or is he trying to achieve something else (if so, what)? Experiment with different ways of playing these lines; for example, in a violent and maniacal way or in a calm and official way. You may find it interesting to compare the way girls and boys tackle these same few lines.

8   Experiment with the delivery of the last line, 'wipe the blood from your hands too'. Can you find a way of delivering this line so that the audience are also made to feel they have blood on their hands and are equally responsible for the girl's death?

Further development

1   In pairs improvise a scene in which A accuses B of throwing a brick through a shop window. B denies this but A has positive proof. For every bit of proof A comes up with B always manages to give an innocent explanation. Keep the improvisation going for as long as you can.

2   Some of the comedy in the scene comes from stating the obvious in a ridiculous way, for example, 'The gun spat metal, a gob of metal which parted her soft tissues. I think it was then she died.' In pairs or small groups invent a scene in which people only say what is absolutely obvious.

3   Another comic moment is when we find out that the killer's name is Bombay Bill, also known as The Slaughterer, and that his address is Skull Lane. As a whole class, set up a party at the annual conference for the 'Society of Those with Names Befitting Their Jobs'.

4   Underlying the comedy one can detect a few serious comments; for example, 'I have slain no-one. It was the gunmaker.' Discuss what you think this comment and the one following it – 'It was the Hebrew who made the law she broke' – might mean. Write or improvise a scene in which someone visits another land in which something that we would consider very wrong is accepted as normal.

5   Experiment with ways of turning a 'normal' conversation into an absurd one. For example, try replacing certain key words with others that don't fit. In a conversation about school the word 'school' could be replaced by the word 'banana'. As you get used to the idea change more and more of the words while keeping the delivery and tone of the conversation 'normal'. Think back to your earlier work on tone of voice and pace in order to make it sound as if the conversation is sensible though the words being spoken are nonsense.

6   As a variant of the technique used in Question 5, try to make a conversation appear absurd and comic by using an inappropriate style of speech. Imagine, for

example, if motor mechanics talked to car owners in the same way as a doctor might talk to the relatives of a dying patient.

7   Although *She's Dead* has a lot of comedy in it, there is something rather nightmarish about it also. What do you normally associate with the idea of 'Hell'? What, on the other hand, would 'Hell' be for you personally? Devise a scene in which a group of criminals arrive in Hell and discover that it is full of things they personally loathe the most.

JOHNSON OVER JORDAN

by J.B. Priestley

CAST (in order of appearance)

CLERK

JOHNSON

FIRST EXAMINER

SECOND EXAMINER

*SECRETARIES AND CLERKS

4 speaking parts. No doubling.
*Non-speaking parts.

Between the two world wars British theatre took on a very conventional air. Although some of the plays written in that period are certainly masterpieces they tend to be so more because of the way they are written rather than the stories they tell or the themes they explore. This was the age of the 'well-made play'. There was little experimentation in form or style and success was measured not in terms of a play's literary quality or the originality of its ideas, but by how well it appealed to West End audiences.

J.B. Priestley was different to the run-of-the-mill playwrights of the time in many respects. While he didn't try to break away from the accepted style of writing, he did try to tackle new ideas and question social responsibility; he frequently lampooned and criticised the behaviour and attitudes of the business-men who would probably have made up most of the audiences in the West End theatres. There is a down-to-earth quality in many of his characters; they seem to represent certain types of people rather than being complex personalities in their own right. Priestley's own radical background made him want audiences to ask themselves questions about the way the world was going. The fact that so much modern British theatre now addresses itself to political and social issues may largely be due to the influence of his work.

Something that interested Priestley immensely was the concept of 'time'. A number of scientists of the period were offering various theories about the actual nature of time and Priestley, in a number of plays such as *Time and the Conways*, tried to show what the implications of these theories were in human terms.

In *Johnson Over Jordan* he explores the possibility of a kind of 'fourth dimension' in which we might exist after death. This spiritual reality is made up of images from an earthly life. Priestley might be suggesting that the key to what our lives mean rests not in our bodily presence but in the impression we leave in other people and what impression they leave in us.

The play starts with Robert Johnson's wife, children and close friends leaving his house to attend his funeral. It then switches into another dimension into which Johnson, unaware of his death, has been projected. Johnson goes on a strange journey during which he meets various characters from his past and is forced to confront his failings in life in order to appreciate the true value of his achievements and so move on to a final state of rest.

The style of the play

Although the play is constructed in a way that audiences in the 1930s were used to, the style of presentation would have been quite a novelty. Priestley's suggestions for the use of sound, light, mask and movement seem to have more similarities with recent experimental theatre than with the usual drawing-room dramas and comedies of the English stage at the time. The action switches through time and space as Johnson embarks on a strange and sometimes scary journey into his own conscience. As a character he is a sort of Everyman – the typical chap – and the people he meets in this world after death are distinct stereotypes.

The extract

Johnson first appears in a tight white spotlight. He is delirious but bit by bit imagines himself to be in his office. As his vision becomes clearer to him so the lights on stage reveal it. However, the office is peopled with clerks and secretaries who go about their business in a kind of manic ballet. A voice booms over the loudspeaker issuing orders to those sitting at desks desperately trying to fill in impossibly difficult forms.

CLERK [*cutting in*]   Here's your form.

> *He hands over the form, then turns away, but this is not good enough for* JOHNSON, *who stops him, not far from one of the big office doors.*

JOHNSON [*with the remnant of his patience*]   Just a moment, please.

CLERK [*unpleasantly*]   We're busy here, you know, very busy. Listen!

> He opens the nearest door, and we hear the clatter of a very large
> office – typewriters, adding machines, ringing of bells, etc. But now
> JOHNSON *really loses his temper.*

JOHNSON [*shouting angrily*]   I don't care how busy you are. I want to
know something.   5

CLERK [*very civil now*]   Certainly, Mr Johnson. What is it?

JOHNSON   I want to know where I am. What *is* this place?

CLERK   Central offices of the Universal Assurance and Globe Loan
and Finance Corporation. Where you get your money.

JOHNSON [*remembering*]   Ah – yes, of course. My money.   10

CLERK [*smiling*]   We all have to have money, haven't we? Can't do
without that.

JOHNSON [*rather confusedly*]   No, of course not. But – the trouble is,
you see – well, I must have lost my memory . . . I've been ill . . . I
was in bed – yes, in a nursing home . . . doctors coming all the time   15
. . . two nurses . . . everybody looking worried . . . I must have
wandered out somehow . . .

CLERK [*with the air of one dealing with a child*]   Quite so. Well, all you
have to do is to fill in your form properly and then we give you your
money. You can't get out of here until you have your money, so of   20
course you have to stay here until you've filled in your form properly.

JOHNSON [*rather dubiously*]   Yes – well – that's reasonable enough.
Filled in plenty of forms in my time – all kinds – [*Glances at the huge
form in his hand.*] Pretty elaborate sort of thing, though – isn't it?
Complicated questions. Is – er – all this necessary?   25

CLERK   Most certainly. You must concentrate, Mr Johnson, concentrate.

JOHNSON   I'll do my best.

CLERK   And our examiners will be here in a moment.

JOHNSON [*who doesn't like the sound of this*]   What examiners?   30

CLERK   For the usual preliminary questions. Meanwhile, Mr Johnson,
I advise you to take a good look at your form.

> He goes out. JOHNSON *walks slowly to the chair at the back of the
> desk, sits down and stares in bewilderment at the pages of complicated
> questions. As he stares he pulls a pipe out and sticks it into his mouth.
> Immediately the voice from the loud-speaker says severely: 'No smok-
> ing in the office before five-fifteen.' After giving the loud-speaker a
> startled glance,* JOHNSON *puts the pipe away. He tries to apply him-*

self to the form, but now the lights change, the ballet of clerks and secretaries comes rushing in, making strange shadows, and we hear again their strident nervous music. When these clerks and secretaries have gone and the brilliant white lights pour down on the desk again, we discover that the EXAMINERS *have arrived, and are standing one on each side of* JOHNSON, *who is still seated. They are exactly alike, these* EXAMINERS, *tall and round figures, dressed in frock-coats, with bald pink heads and round pink shaven faces and large spectacles. They carry notebooks.* JOHNSON *looks at them in astonishment touched with horror, as well he might.*

FIRST EXAMINER [*announcing himself*]   First Examiner.

SECOND EXAMINER [*announcing himself*]   Second Examiner.

FIRST EXAMINER   Robert Johnson?   35

JOHNSON   Yes.

SECOND EXAMINER [*glancing at his notes*]   Born in Grantham Street, Longfield?

JOHNSON   Yes.

FIRST EXAMINER [*reading from his notes*]   Elder son of Frederick   40
Johnson, solicitor's clerk, who for more than ten years sacrificed a number of personal comforts and pleasures in order to give you a good education?

JOHNSON [*staggered*]   Yes, I suppose he did. He – was a good father.

SECOND EXAMINER   Did you ever thank him for those sacrifices?   45

JOHNSON [*rather shamefaced*]   No. And I ought to have done.

SECOND EXAMINER [*referring to his notes*]   Your mother, Edith Johnson, I see, died of peritonitis at a comparatively early age. She was warned that an operation was necessary but refused to have one in time because she was afraid of the expense and the trouble it would   50
cause her husband and children. You knew that, of course?

JOHNSON [*deeply troubled*]   No – I didn't. I – I sometimes wondered – that's all.

FIRST EXAMINER [*glancing at his notebook, relentlessly*]   And yet you
have referred to yourself at times, I see, as a good son.   55

JOHNSON [*thoroughly uncomfortable*]   I only meant – well – we all seemed to get on together, y'know – not like some families. They were very decent to me. I've always admitted that. [*Hesitantly.*] As a matter of fact, I've been thinking about all that . . . just lately . . . I remember, just after I was taken ill –   60

SECOND EXAMINER [*briskly*]   Yes now – you were taken ill.

JOHNSON [*brightening up, for we are all proud of our illnesses*]   Yes. Quite suddenly. A most extraordinary thing – but –

FIRST EXAMINER [*cutting in, ruthlessly*] You have occupied a responsible position for some time? 65

JOHNSON [*bewildered and rather sulky*] Yes, I suppose so.

SECOND EXAMINER [*severely*] You are a husband – and a father?

JOHNSON Yes.

FIRST EXAMINER [*severely*] What care have you taken of your health?

JOHNSON [*apologetically*] Well – I've always tried – 70

FIRST EXAMINER [*ignoring him*] The heart, the lungs, the liver and kidneys, the digestive system, the intestinal tract.

SECOND EXAMINER The abdominal wall must be firm – no sagging.

FIRST EXAMINER [*who now sits on the desk, facing* JOHNSON] The teeth need the greatest care. Particles of decaying food lodged in dental 75 cavities may produce a septic condition.

SECOND EXAMINER [*also sitting*] Eye-strain is common among sedentary workers. How often have you given yourself a boracic eyebath or had your sight examined?

FIRST EXAMINER Alcohol and rich starchy foods must be avoided. 80 Have you avoided them?

SECOND EXAMINER Smoking leads to nicotine poisoning and may easily ruin the digestion.

FIRST EXAMINER Everywhere you go, you risk infection.

SECOND EXAMINER But the common cold, the beginning of many serious 85 ailments, may be traced to a lack of fresh air.

FIRST EXAMINER Few of us take the trouble to walk properly.

SECOND EXAMINER Or to sit properly. You should always sit upright, not allowing the spine to be curved. Learn to sit properly.

> The wretched JOHNSON, *who has been slumped deep into his chair, now sharply raises himself to a more erect position, but it does not help him.*

FIRST EXAMINER But take care to relax. The nervous strain of modern 90 life demands constant and complete relaxation. Loosen those tense muscles.

JOHNSON [*slumping again, but determined to protest at last*] Now – look here – just a minute – !

SECOND EXAMINER [*very severely, rising*] Please – we have no time to 95 waste.

> The two monsters *make rapid and contemptuous notes in their books, while* JOHNSON *regards them helplessly.*

FIRST EXAMINER You owe it to yourself, to your wife and family, to your employer and fellow workers, to your country, to take sufficient exercise.

JOHNSON [*who mistakenly feels on safe ground here*]   I've always enjoyed   100
taking exercise. Tennis and golf –

SECOND EXAMINER [*very severely*]   Too many middle-aged men, sedentary workers, imagine that they can improve their physical condition
by rushing into games at the week-end, and only succeed in strain-
ing their hearts.   105

JOHNSON [*desperately*]   I've tried not to overdo it, and every morning,
if it wasn't too late, I did a few exercises in my bedroom –

FIRST EXAMINER [*very severely*]   Nearly all systems of home exercises,
devised by professional strong men without expert physiological
knowledge, are liable to do more harm than good.   110

SECOND EXAMINER   Consult your doctor first. *He* knows.

FIRST EXAMINER   But the habit of flying to the doctor on every trivial
occasion is dangerous and must be avoided.

JOHNSON [*sinking fast now*]   Look here, gentlemen, all I can say is –
I've tried to do my best.   115

SECOND EXAMINER [*going right up to him, in smooth deadly tone*]
Possibly. But is your best good enough?

FIRST EXAMINER [*with the same horrible technique*]   After all, what do
you know?

SECOND EXAMINER [*severe again now*]   How far have you tried to   120
acquaint yourself with the findings of chemistry, physics, biology,
ecology, astronomy, mathematics?

FIRST EXAMINER   Ask yourself what you know about the Mendelian
Law, the Quantum Theory, Spectral analysis, or the behaviour of
Electrons and Neutrons.   125

SECOND EXAMINER   Could you explain Freud's theory of the Id, Marx's
Surplus Value, Neo-Realism, Non-representational Art, Polyphonic
Music?

FIRST EXAMINER   Or – give an exact account of the sequence of events
leading up to the outbreak of war in 1914?   130

SECOND EXAMINER [*with dangerous easiness*]   You were taught French
at school?

JOHNSON   Yes.

SECOND EXAMINER [*turning like a tiger*]   Have you ever brushed up your
French?   135

JOHNSON [*desperately*]   No, but I've always been meaning to. Hang it!
– a man can't do everything –

FIRST EXAMINER [*calmly and maddeningly*]   A postman in South-East
London taught himself to speak eight foreign languages fluently in
his spare time.   140

SECOND EXAMINER [*in the same tone*]   A cinema operator in Pasa-
dena, California, recently received an honours degree in natural
sciences.

JOHNSON [*wearily, almost brokenly*]   I know, I know. And good luck to
them. But as I told you –   145

FIRST EXAMINER [*very severely*]   Kindly tell us what we ask you to tell
us. We have no time now for general conversation. You have two
children?

JOHNSON [*brightening up, for this may let him out*]   Yes. A boy and a girl.

SECOND EXAMINER   You are fond of them?   150

JOHNSON [*indignantly*]   Of course I am.

FIRST EXAMINER   What serious thought have you ever given to their
education, to their mental development, to their emotional and
spiritual life?

SECOND EXAMINER   They are the citizens of the future, the inheritors   155
of a great empire –

JOHNSON   I know, I know. I've often thought of that.

SECOND EXAMINER [*pressing him*]   Really thought about it, or merely,
after an unnecessarily heavy meal accompanied by alcohol, con-
gratulated yourself that these children were an extension of your   160
own ego?

FIRST EXAMINER   You have helped to bring them into this world, but
what kind of world have you brought them into?

JOHNSON [*hastily, hoping he is now on firmer ground*]   Oh – well – I've
no illusions about that –   165

SECOND EXAMINER [*angrily*]   We are not asking you about your illusions. For many years now you have had a vote?

JOHNSON [*still hoping*]   Yes, and I've always used it – not like some
chaps –

FIRST EXAMINER   But how much of your time and serious attention   170
have been given to the problems that must be studied by a wise
member of the electorate?

SECOND EXAMINER   For example, the Gold Standard as against an artificial currency based on the balance of trade. The relations between
nationalism and Tariffs. The fallacy of colonial exploitation.   175

FIRST EXAMINER   What account of any value could you give of the
political significance of minorities in Central Europe, the impor-
tance of the Ukraine in European affairs, the success or failure of
Stalin's second Five Year Plan?

SECOND EXAMINER   Could you define accurately Facism?   180

FIRST EXAMINER   National Socialism?

SECOND EXAMINER   Russian Communism?

JOHNSON [*a rebel at last, jumping up*]   No. Could you? [*As they do not reply, but make notes.*] I might as well tell you, I've had enough of this. Who are you, anyhow? [*As they do not reply, but look at each other significantly.*] I don't even know why I'm here. Loss of memory – or something. No reason why I should stay.   185

FIRST EXAMINER [*ignoring this outburst*]   Your form, please.

> *He takes the form, hastily makes some marks on it, then hands it back.*

JOHNSON [*angrily*]   I don't want the thing.

> JOHNSON *throws the form on the table and sits sulking. The two* EXAMINERS *look at the form, then at him, give a nod to each other, and go off through one of the big office doors.*

JOHNSON   I'm not staying, y'know. Why should I? I didn't want to come here. Keep your money.   190

> *But the* EXAMINER *has gone.* JOHNSON *sits slumped in his chair behind the desk, a sulky rebel.*

Understanding the text

1   List three things in the extract that suggest the scene is not taking place in the real world.

2   What sort of person do you imagine Johnson to be? Write brief notes describing any faults and qualities that you think he has. (For example, he seems to be quite impatient at first.) Add what you think his main likes, dislikes, hobbies and habits might be (judging from this first introduction).

3   The Examiners disturb Johnson with their questions. Which appear to worry him the most? What might this suggest about his character?

4   Johnson looks rather small and foolish in this scene. Apart from the difficult questions he is asked, what other things make him appear so?

Producing the scene

1   Write out a list of all the sound effects actually demanded in the script and suggest more if you think they are appropriate. Experiment with ways of making some of the sounds.

2   In places the stage directions suggest music. Could you suggest any music you know which might be suitable? Actually recording a sound track for this scene could be an unusual and interesting project.

3   How might you create the strange shadows suggested in the long stage direction, and generally make the 'office' seem nightmarish by using the lighting equipment you have available? If you know of the existence of other types of lights that you could hire, consider them also.

4   Finding two people who look exactly alike to play the Examiners could be a considerable problem. One solution which would also add to the strangeness of the scene might be to make identical masks.

- Jot down some ideas about the type of characters the Examiners seem to have.
- Design a caricature which reflects their attitudes.

5   By acting out the scene, try to find ways for the Examiners to make Johnson feel small and uncomfortable by the way they move around him during the 'interrogation'. Write a stage direction which describes how they should move.

6   Do you think the Examiners ought to ask their questions at a steady, even pace all the way through the scene, or should they increase the pace? Experiment with both methods and note the different qualities of each before making your final choice.

7   At the end of the scene Johnson starts to stick up for himself by shouting at the Examiners. However, they have already gone and so the gesture is rather wasted. How could you make Johnson's rebellion look totally futile on stage? Consider how you could achieve this through lighting, position on stage, gesture and facial expression.

Further development

1   You might have heard it said that your whole life flashes in front of you when you're drowning. In groups of about six improvise, at breakneck speed and off the tops of your heads, someone's life from birth to death.

2   In *Johnson Over Jordan*, Johnson re-encounters several characters from his past life whom he has cause to remember. In groups of four or five (more if you think you can manage) prepare a programme set in the next world called 'Robert Johnson, This WAS Your Life!' You may choose to introduce only two or three characters in the programme.

3   Write or improvise a story in which a person who has died must resolve a piece of 'unfinished business' on earth before she is allowed to move on to her final resting place.

4   Get into pairs and label yourselves A and B. A starts a spontaneous

improvisation by taking Johnson's lines, 'I've been ill . . . I must have wandered out somehow . . .'. Work on this for no more than one minute and then start a new scene in which B says these lines. Generate as many different quick-fire scenes as you can, always using this same starting line. Which one struck you as having most potential? Try to script it or develop it through further improvisation.

5   Working in groups of three improvise an interrogation session in which the aim is not so much to find out information from the 'victim' as to confuse and frustrate her totally. Try to make use of the following techniques:

- varying the speed of the questions
- moving round the person
- changing the tone and volume of your voices
- changing the characters of the interrogators

and do anything else that will make it difficult for the victim to concentrate. After a few minutes choose a new person to be the victim so you all have a chance to play both roles. Talk about both how you personally felt about the experience and about ways of turning that into a piece of carefully prepared theatre afterwards.

6   Improvise a scene in which a number of ghosts are returning home, wherever they might be, after a hard night's haunting. How could you develop the idea that they have been able to see and touch living people without being seen themselves? What would make it a 'hard night's haunting'?

7   If you have access to sound and lighting equipment, devise a way of using it to produce an 'atmosphere' which could be used at the opening of a play to suggest something eerie.

THE GUT GIRLS

by *Sarah Daniels*

CAST (in order of appearance)

POLLY

KATE

ANNIE

MAGGIE

LADY HELENA

PRISCILLA

EDWIN

7 speaking parts.

Sarah Daniels is a playwright whose work has focused on the abuse of women and the violence done against them. She became recognised as one of Britain's leading playwrights during the 1980s. At the time, Britain had its first woman Prime Minister – Margaret Thatcher. However, like a number of other playwrights Sarah Daniels recognised that Thatcherite politics seemed both to encourage women to play an active part in the economy but also promoted attitudes which were critical of them. During this period the government strongly supported a return to the 'Victorian values' of loyalty and devotion to one's family and a respect for one's employers. However, the government's critics pointed out that Victorian Britain was also characterised by a divide between the 'haves', who looked on the outside to be thoroughly respectable while doing pretty much what they liked in private, and the 'have-nots' who were expected to 'put up and shut up'. Women in Victorian England had a particularly bad time of it. The expectation was that they should do whatever men told them to do, and they had little or no power to fight against this. Any women who showed strength of character and the slightest independence could expect to be reviled and regarded as having no morals.

The Gut Girls is set in Victorian England. It tells the story of a group of women who worked in a slaughterhouse in south London. Their job was, literally, to take all the guts out of the slaughtered cattle in preparation for them to be jointed ready for the butchers' shops. It was hard and filthy work. The only way the women could manage was to become hard themselves – they had little choice. The alternative was to give up their independence and go into 'service' where, as lowly maids, they were often treated as little better than slaves. The play largely focuses on Annie, a sixteen year old who is forced to go to work in the gutting sheds. Having worked as a maid she was thrown out of the household when she became pregnant after being raped by her employer's son. On her first day at work, the gutting shed is visited by Lady Helena, a duchess who is set on trying to 'improve' the working women by setting up a club for them. The gut girls are reluctant to go along and resentful of the way in which the duchess starts to use the club as a means of training them for domestic service when the slaughterhouse is forced to shut down the gutting sheds. Having learned that they can look after themselves and defy men and women such as Lady Helena who want to keep things as they are, the gut girls find it hard to fit back into 'accepted society'. For some, the transition has tragic consequences, while other become more determined than ever to fight for their rights.

The style of the play

The Gut Girls is based on a real incident but it is not a piece of documentary theatre. Although there really was a Duchess of Albany who set up a club for the gut girls in Deptford, the characters in the play have been constructed by Sarah Daniels in order to make a point about the way Victorian society treated women. Underlying the play is the suggestion that some of the attitudes towards women then had not changed much by the 1980s. The gut girls are tough and may seem coarse but they are also supportive of each other, intelligent and witty. They are down to earth and fiercely independent; what you see is what you get. This contrasts with the duplicity of the gentry. Lady Helena has her own reasons for setting up the club. Priscilla hides her secret that she is beaten by her husband who owns the gutting sheds, and while Edwin looks like a gentleman he certainly doesn't behave like one. These contrasts need to be shown very clearly in order for the play to make its point.

The extract

The two scenes presented here demonstrate the differences between the gut girls and the gentry. In the first scene Lady Helena is trying to 'educate' the girls to make them acceptable in her society. But this means they will not only have to change the way they speak and behave but give up all of the things that have helped them survive so far in a tough world. In the second scene we see why those survival tactics are so important and what the dangers of submitting to Lady Helena's values would be for the girls.

Part two
Scene one

> *The club is a complete contrast to the shed. It is clean, clinical, sparse and quiet.* POLLY, KATE, ANNIE *and* MAGGIE *sit at desks, sewing knickers for themselves.*

LADY HELENA   Quiet please.

> *The room falls to hush.* LADY HELENA *goes over to* PRISCILLA.

PRISCILLA   It was an excellent idea to allow them to leave work an hour early. The place is full to overflowing every week.

LADY HELENA   Unfortunately, the majority of them are still extremely unwilling to learn. Immediate gratification is the name of their   5
game. Can't see the value of what they will achieve in the long run.

PRISCILLA   Give them a few more weeks.

LADY HELENA   But in the meantime. I'm afraid of losing their interest so I've asked Edwin to pop in with a surprise.

PRISCILLA   Oh?   10

> *While* LADY HELENA *and* PRISCILLA *have their backs turned the girls start to whisper to each other.*

ANNIE   I can't understand Ellen. Still not coming here, even with an hour off.

MAGGIE   Except that we have to stay for three hours in total and it's worse than school.

KATE   It's not hard work though is it?   15

MAGGIE   At least me Mum don't give me no aggravation 'bout coming here. She's well pleased me and Lady Helena are breathing the same air. What's the matter with you Pol, lost yer tongue?

POLLY   I'm trying to finish me fucking knickers ain't I.

ANNIE   What's so special 'bout your fanny?   20

MAGGIE [*shocked*]   Annie, really. Try and remember you're a young lady.

KATE   Here Polly, I dare you to call Lady Helena, Lena.

POLLY   I dare you to try her hat on.

KATE   Call that a hat, looks more like a frozen cow turd.   25

LADY HELENA   Girls, girls, your attention please, you are here to learn not chatter.

MAGGIE [*to the others*]   Wait for it, she's now going to make up a new rule.

ANNIE   D'you remember the first time, when she said there'd be no 30 rules.

KATE   Yeah, now there's about twenty.

LADY HELENA   I will not tolerate talking whilst I'm talking, it is extremely bad manners.

POLLY   Look, Miss, I've finished. [*She holds up an enormous pair of* 35 *bloomers with about eight pockets, all shaped like pork chops or some recognisable piece of meat.*]

MAGGIE   Creep.

LADY HELENA [*walking over to her*]   We usually wait till we're asked but [*Looking at the knickers.*] you have done well. I didn't expect anyone 40 to finish until next week at least. Are you sure they're not a little on the large side? And, good gracious me, all these pockets. What on earth?

POLLY   Hankies, Miss. We need a lot of them. Don't do ter go wiping yer nose on yer hand. Knife would slip right outta it. 45

LADY HELENA   Now where was I.

POLLY   Oh, Lena.

LADY HELENA   I beg your pardon.

POLLY [*holds up the knickers*]   You meant I was leaner. I've made these too big. Was that what you was meaning? 50

LADY HELENA   Oh I see. [*Looking at* POLLY.] It is quite possible I was mistaken. Now I would like, with your consent of course, to introduce a new rule.

KATE [*to* POLLY]   Dare you to call her Hell then.

POLLY   Give over, you got to try her hat on first. 55

LADY HELENA [*talking over them*]   This new rule is that no loose women should be allowed to come to the club.

KATE   We don't know what you mean Mam.

MAGGIE [*to* ANNIE]   Don't worry, we won't say nothing. Don't say nothing. 60

POLLY   I know I could be leaner but [*Holding up her arm.*] this is all muscle. May look loose but honest, Miss, it's muscle.

LADY HELENA   Those who have strayed from the path of virtue.

MAGGIE   Which side of Evelyn Street is that on?

LADY HELENA [*deep breath*]   I meant fallen women. 65

POLLY [*trips and falls on the floor*]   Oh blimey, what am I going to do, I've fallen.

The others slips off their chairs.

MAGGIE   Oh no, we're all fallen women.

LADY HELENA   That's quite enough. All of you get up this instant, put your sewing away and sit, hands in laps. It's time for the Bible read- 70 ing. [*She opens the Bible trying to find her place.*] Ah, here we are. Now I've found something very relevant and something I think you'll find very interesting because it's directly connected to St. Nicholas's church which is the church just around the corner from where you work. Now who can tell me what it's got on its gate posts? 75

MAGGIE [*mutters*]   Dog shit.

KATE [*calls out*]   Two skulls.

LADY HELENA   Quite right. And does anyone know why?

POLLY [*calls out*]   Two heads is better than one Miss?

LADY HELENA   That's as maybe, but these two have biblical signifi- 80 cance. Can anyone tell me what it is?

MAGGIE [*calls out*]   To remind us that there's more dead people in the world than live ones.

LADY HELENA   In fact not, no. They resemble a vision Ezekiel was given by God. And I'm going to read it to you. Now the language is 85 rather antiquated and cumbersome so bear with me whilst I para- phrase for your benefit.

ANNIE [*mutters*]   Wake me up when it's time to go to the pub.

> LADY HELENA *has to look down to do this. Consequently she can't see them all messing about.* KATE *immediately gets up and stands behind her, puts her hat on and starts mimicking.*

LADY HELENA   Ezekiel Chapter 47. I felt the powerful presence of the Lord. He took me to the valley of dry bones. He said to me 'Can 90 these bones come back to life?' I replied 'Lord only you can answer that'. He said 'Tell these dry bones to listen to the work of God. Tell them I am the sovereign Lord', and thus said the Lord God 'behold I will come, breathe life into you and you shall live. I will give you muscles and cover you with skin and cause your blood to flow'. 95

> KATE *quickly replaces the hat, the girls applaud.*

LADY HELENA   I'm pleased you enjoyed that, but we don't usually clap at the Bible. Still I particularly like that passage myself.

MAGGIE   Oh Miss, excuse me, but where we come from 'passage' is a rude word.

LADY HELENA   Can anyone tell me what it means. 100

KATE   Well, it's like your 'underneath': yer privates.

LADY HELENA   No. The reading from the Bible, can anyone tell me what they think the significance is.

POLLY   Hell?

LADY HELENA   What did you say?   105

POLLY   Isn't it like a vision of hell, everything dried up and that.

LADY HELENA   Oh I see. Yes, well done, Polly. It is sort of but with a
happy ending and shall I tell you why I like it?

MAGGIE [*mumbles*]   Do we have the power to stop you?

LADY HELENA   Because it's what I see today in Deptford. Young people   110
like yourselves, all dried up without hope and future. But it doesn't
have to be like that.

MAGGIE [*mutters*]   Bleedin' arrogance of the silly mare.

POLLY   Maybe she means the sheep girls.

MAGGIE   I don't care who she means. If anybody needs to dry up   115
should be her.

LADY HELENA   Now next week is Holy Week.

KATE [*to* MAGGIE]   No such luck.

LADY HELENA   Who knows what Holy Week is about?

MAGGIE   Having a good time.   120

LADY HELENA   It is not. It is remembering that Jesus died and suffered
for each and everyone one of us. But . . .

POLLY   Who?

LADY HELENA   Our Lord, Jesus Christ.

MAGGIE   Never heard of him.   125

   Chorus of 'No'.

KATE   Yes, you have. They're being silly Miss. We learnt it at school,
he was the one what gave someone a kiss.

LADY HELENA   Well, I can't quite recall.

POLLY   Nelson, that's right.

LADY HELENA   Goodness me, that's . . . Come on now you must know   130
who. [*She sees* EDWIN *come in.*] Excuse me a moment.

ANNIE [*to others*]   Don't keep this up. Now we'll get the life story of
Jesus.

MAGGIE [*to* ANNIE]   I wouldn't fret. We was going to get it anyway.

LADY HELENA   Listen, listen. This evening we have a special treat.   135
Something that I'm sure will amaze you. Lord Tartaden very kindly
agreed to come along this evening with a lantern slide and we will
be able to see details from our Lord's life with the aid of magic.

   EDWIN *sets it up. The girls show genuine interest for the first time,*
   never having seen a lantern slide show before, it must seem like magic
   to them.

EDWIN   All set.

LADY HELENA   Perhaps you'd be so good as to take us through.   140

> EDWIN *decides to charm the girls by being skittish.*

EDWIN   Right ho. [*Picture of Jesus in the manger.*] Here we have a picture of Jesus in the first perambulator ever invented. It wasn't until
some years later that they decided to put wheels on it.

LADY HELENA [*hisses*]   This is supposed to be educational, Edwin.
[*Then to the girls.*] This picture shows that the Son of God started   145
life in very humble surroundings.

EDWIN   Here we have spouting – er– teaching in the temple, aged
twelve. Then a little gap in the story 'til we find him here on the
cross. [*Picture of the crucifixion.*] What a way to spend Easter eh?

LADY HELENA   He died so that we might know too of the life hereafter,   150
to let us know that we all have a choice here on earth to be born
again, a fresh start. Lord Tartaden, do you have the picture of the
stone being rolled away?

EDWIN   Umm, let's see now. Oh yes, well, there's one of him making
his first public appearance after the crucifixion to old Mary   155
Magdalene.

LADY HELENA   Ah, now she is a very important character, and one of
my favourites amongst the women in the New Testament. This
Mary, unlike the mother of God, was shunned by those around her.
She was coarse and led a heathen, contemptuous way of life, but   160
Jesus didn't judge her. He went out of His way to get to know her
and through Him her life was completely transformed.

MAGGIE [*to others*]   What's she getting at?

ANNIE [*shrugs*]   Search me.

LADY HELENA   Now please dismiss quietly, and remember to behave   165
with social manners, not only whilst in this room but in the street,
and in your work. This week I want you to take our Lord Jesus home
with you. I'll see you all next week at eight o'clock prompt.

> *They start to put their hats and coats on.* EDWIN *goes over to* HELENA
> *and helps her on with her coat.*

POLLY [*unseen, except by* MAGGIE, *carefully takes the slide of Jesus and puts
it in her pocket*]   Come on Jesus.   170

MAGGIE [*hisses*]   What you doing?

POLLY [*shrugs*]   She said we had to tek Jesus home with us.

MAGGIE   C'mon, let's get outta here.

> *They all rush out laughing, screaming and shouting.*

LADY HELENA [*sighs, puts her hand to her forehead*]   Little more than
    riotous beasts.   175
EDWIN [*with enthusiasm*]   Rather. [*Then.*] I mean high-spirited coltish-
    ness.
LADY HELENA   Magic lantern was a great success. Many thanks, Tarty.
EDWIN   Don't mention it. I must be off. [*He kisses her on the cheek.*]
LADY HELENA   Edwin.   180
EDWIN   Wishful thinking, wishful thinking. [*He goes.*]
LADY HELENA   Well, Priscilla, we certainly have our work cut out.
PRISCILLA [*collects the undergarments*]   There's one pair missing.
LADY HELENA   That one, Polly, finished hers. I was quite astounded.
    She shows precious little interest in anything else.   185
PRISCILLA   But she hasn't paid for them.
LADY HELENA   We'll see her next week. Don't worry. Maybe we should
    try and extend the activities of the sewing class. Poor children have
    such disgusting clothes.
PRISCILLA   That awful, gaudy jewellery and those hideous hats.   190

Scene two

    In the street.

MAGGIE   What I can't understand is them having all that money and
    wearing such awful clothes.
POLLY   That hat. Fancy wearing it. I wouldn't be caught dead being
    seen in something like that in the street.
KATE   If she'd 'ave caught me wearing it I'd only be half alive.   195
ANNIE   I ain't going next week.
MAGGIE   Listen Annie, don't take it to heart, that rubbish about fallen
    women. She don't know anything 'bout yer and she ain't going ter
    find out neither.
ANNIE   But that ain't the point is it. Anyway, I can't work out what   200
    she's bothering with us for in the first place.
POLLY   She wants to turn us into real ladies, don't she.
MAGGIE   You lot are getting as bad as old po-faced Ellen, you are. And
    I've got to get home, otherwise I'll get it off old misery chops.
POLLY   She ain't that bad, yer Mum.   205
MAGGIE   You don't know her like I do.
ANNIE   We'll walk yer to the bottom of Evelyn Street.
MAGGIE   Don't worry, I'm not so much of a lady yet to be worried
    about a few drunks. See yer tomorrow.
POLLY   Night.   210

    MAGGIE *walks on alone. She thinks she can hear something. Looks back. Nothing there. Walks on.* EDWIN *suddenly steps out of the shadows blocking her path.*

EDWIN   Good evening young lady.

MAGGIE   [*levelly*]   Evening sir. [*She steps to one side. He steps in front of her. She looks at him.*] Mind if I get on me way.

EDWIN   You've got time to stop and talk with a gentleman, just for a while, haven't you?   215

MAGGIE   No, please let me pass.

EDWIN   [*takes her arm*]   How would you like to earn a shilling?

MAGGIE   [*removes his hand. Nervous*]   Don't touch what you can't afford sir.

EDWIN   Oh, but I can afford anything I want.   220

MAGGIE   I just want to get home. Please get out of my way.

EDWIN   I only want a few moments of your time.

MAGGIE   I said no sir, now.

EDWIN   [*pushing her. Suddenly produces a small pocket knife and points it at her*]   Now this is not the way I normally like to conduct business,   225
but you leave me very little option.

MAGGIE   [*steps back. Looks at him*]   I work all day with these. [*She gracefully pulls out a large knife from her skirts.*] So don't make me laugh wiv that plaything. [*She brings her knife down and knocks it from his hand.*] And if you don't want ter see yer wedding tackle on sale   230
in Wellbeloved's tomorrow – fer less than a shilling no doubt – I'd scarper and sharpish [*Prods him.*] mate.

EDWIN   [*backing off*]   I'll get you for this, you slut. Don't think I don't know who you are, where you work. I'll find yer. Next time darling, next time.   235

He goes. She watches him. He breaks into a run. She into a sweat.

Understanding the text

1   Although Lady Helena appears to be trying to help the 'gut girls', what evidence is there in this extract to suggest that she neither really cares about or likes them? Pick out at least three lines that you think reveal her real attitude towards the girls.

2   Priscilla's line, 'It was an excellent idea to allow them to leave work an hour early. The place is full to overflowing every week' suggests that the girls only go to the club because it is a better alternative to spending an extra hour in the

gutting sheds. How would you describe their attitude towards Lady Helena, though? Find examples of things they do and say that reveal what they think and feel about her.

3   The way the gut girls talk is very different from the way Lady Helena and Priscilla talk. Most obviously, their choice of words (vocabulary) is different, but look also at the way the sentences are structured. Divide a sheet of paper into three columns and two rows. Label the first column 'Style of Language'. In the first row, jot down words and phrases that help to describe the *way* the gut girls speak. In the second row do the same for the ladies. Mark the second column 'Examples' and under this heading jot down four or five things that either the gut girls or the ladies say that seem to be 'typical' of them. Give the third column the heading 'Notes on Delivery' and try here to describe how actors playing the parts should use their voices to capture the characters. Think about tone of voice, pace, volume and where in the mouth or throat the sounds would come from (the best way to find out, of course, is to try saying your sample lines).

4   How would you describe Edwin as a character? Why do you think he has agreed to go to the club in the first place? Does he share Lady Helena's values towards the girls – if so, which ones? Why do you imagine that he thinks he can treat Maggie in the way he does?

5   What major issues seem to be explored in this short extract? Although *The Gut Girls* is set in Victorian England, do you think that it still has relevance today?

Producing the scene

1   What particular demands are made in this extract that will be important to the set designer? Make a list of all of the things that you feel it is very important for an audience to be able to witness in the extract. Include specific actions and moments when you would want the audience to be able to notice a particular character's facial expression (for example, when Lady Helena proclaims that there should be no 'loose women' allowed in the club, the audience will be keen to see Annie's reaction as they will know that she has had an illegitimate baby).

2   Draw a plan view of what your set for this extract would be and make four copies of it. Choose four key moments, such as the ones listed in the previous exercise, and show where you would position the actors so that the audience could study the stage picture carefully. Be sure to make it clear which way the actors should be facing and use annotations to suggest what they should be doing at the given moment.

3   The girls take some delight in mocking Lady Helena's hat; Kate describes it as looking like 'a frozen cow turd'. At the end of the scene, though, Priscilla similarly comments on the way the girls are dressed. Research into what sort of

costumes working girls and fine ladies would have worn around 150 years ago and make notes on how you would dress the characters in this play to show the contrast in their lives.

4   It will no doubt take the actor playing Edwin a little while to set up the magic lantern slide show. What do you think the other characters on stage should be doing while he does this? In groups, rehearse some 'stage business' that could go on that could reveal what the girls think of Edwin and the magic lantern at this moment in the play, what he thinks of them and what Lady Helena's attitude to the situation might be. You will need to think about exactly what facial expressions and gestures you want the audience to see here and position the actors carefully. (You may also like to think about how you would be able to produce the slide show. Would you try to make modern, available equipment look like a Victorian magic lantern? Or could you find another way round the problem?)

5   After her friends have left her in Scene Two, we are told that Maggie 'walks on alone. She thinks she can hear something. Looks back. Nothing there. Walks on.' She is then accosted by Edwin. In groups of three, talk about what you imagine city streets in Victorian England to have been like at night. Perhaps you have seen films or plays such as *Dr Jekyll and Mr Hyde* or documentaries about Jack the Ripper. Rehearse this moment on stage, concentrating on timing and movement and culminating with Edwin's line, 'Good evening young lady.' The effect you should try to achieve is one of rising tension and threat – if it's not quite right what you will get is laughter! Make a note also about how you would light this scene to add to the dramatic tension.

Further development

1   A good deal of the comedy in Scene One comes from the way Lady Helena treats the girls and the way they respond. Although she seems to think that the girls are rather stupid they no doubt find her very patronising and set about making fun of her (though she doesn't seem to realise they are doing this). In groups, devise a scene of your own in which someone 'sets themselves up' for mockery because of the high-handed attitude they have towards others.

2   Lady Helena notes that Mary was 'coarse and led a heathen way of life', but that Jesus 'went out of his way to get to know her' and this changed her. It's interesting that she describes Mary as one of her favourites among the women in the Bible because Mary Magdalene, being a prostitute, would certainly not have been welcome in her club! In Scene Two, Edwin certainly goes out of his way to try get to know Maggie, but his assumption that she is a 'loose woman' is completely wrong. The reference to Mary Magdalene illustrates Lady Helena's moralistic viewpoint which is later undermined by her friend Edwin's action. Devise

two scenes of your own. In the first scene some characters adopt a strong moral position on something but in the second scene we should see them do or say something that clearly shows that they have 'double standards'.

3   How might Edwin go about 'getting' Maggie? Do you think he will be successful? In groups, improvise the following three possibilities and compare how the situations are likely to change what the characters say and do:

• It is the following week. Lady Helena and Priscilla are commenting on Maggie's sewing work to her. Edwin enters and is invited to make his comment on Maggie's work also. What happens next?

• Maggie and some of her friends see Edwin talking to another young woman in an alleyway. She looks uncomfortable and he appears to be stopping her from going on her way. What do they do?

• Edwin is lying in wait for Maggie, knowing which way she goes home and at what time. As she approaches, he steps out in front of her again.

Which of your improvised scenes do you think would be: (a) most interesting to act; (b) the most 'dramatic'; (c) add to the overall message of the play?

4   The slaughterhouse that the gut girls work in is closed down. In pairs, improvise a scene in which one of them is being interviewed for a job as a maid by either Lady Helena, Priscilla or Edwin. Make it clear, through the way the interviewer asks questions, what their character and attitude towards the girl is. Share some examples of these improvisations and see if the audience can tell which of the three characters is doing the interviewing.

5   Imagine a time ten or twenty years after the time in which the play is set. In pairs, prepare two contrasting monologues, one for Lady Helena and one for either Maggie or Annie, which illustrate how their lives have changed. How would they remember the club and the slaughterhouse and what happened during those times? Find a way of cutting from one monologue to the other so as to make the characters' contrasting stories dramatically effective.

THE LUCKY ONES

by Tony Marchant

CAST (in order of appearance)

DAVE

TIMOTHY

DEBBIE

JOE

LAWRENCE

5 speaking parts. No doubling.

Writing plays about contemporary issues is a dangerous business. Theatres are often worried about putting anything on that seems 'political' or critical of a society which they rely on for business. Another problem for the writer is that if the play is specifically about one aspect of current life, then it is unlikely to be performed much in the future because it might be seen as irrelevant. Fortunately, there are some theatre companies that will take a chance and put on such plays, and sometimes they are also published, which improves their chance of being performed more widely.

With its underlying theme of mass unemployment, *The Lucky Ones* was very much a play of its time (it was written in 1982). However, one can see in it universal themes and problems; for example, the question of how to get on in the world; does one stand up and fight for one's rights or keep out of the way and hope that one will be rewarded for doing so?

The Lucky Ones is set in the basement of an office building. The four main characters are clearing out boxes of old files. It is a boring and mindless job for which they are paid little. Dave is resentful of the way in which the company treats them as cheap labour. He likens life to a vending machine which won't give anything after you've put your money in: 'Some people smash the machine to bits but they get arrested. Some people are luckier and manage to negotiate a packet of Wrigley's which is not what they wanted at all, but they're thankful for whatever the machine is kind enough to let them have.' He is supported to some extent by Debbie who, as a girl, has the additional problem of being leered at by some of the managers and seen as an object rather than a person. Timothy has a different approach. 'Be acceptable' is his advice to Joe who has just joined the firm and is hoping to make enough money to get married and settle down with his girlfriend, Sandra.

The test of loyalty to the firm comes when the young staff are asked to act as waiters outside office hours at an evening presentation to the firm's managing director.

The style of the play

In a sense *The Lucky Ones* has a quite traditional style in that it tells a story in a straightforward, sequenced way. At the beginning the characters are introduced and the main incident occurs, we then see how the characters react to the incident, and finally see what happens to them because of the way they reacted. It is a 'naturalistic' type of play in that it tries to capture on stage the words and actions of recognisable characters in a believable way. The language of the play is similarly realistic and attempts to reflect how many young people talk to each other when they are together.

The extract

This is a scene from the middle of the play. Dave, Debbie, Joe and Timothy have already been asked to contribute towards buying a present for their boss, Mr Gulley. Now they have been asked to act as waiters at the presentation. They divide into those who want to take a 'militant' line in an attempt to preserve their dignity, and those who will go along with the plan because they think that is the safer and wiser thing to do.

Scene five

    DAVE, JOE, DEBBIE and TIMOTHY *are in the middle of a conversation.*

DAVE   Well, it's a liberty if you ask me. Talk about wringing out the last few drops. He'll come down and give us a fitting for a ball and chain next. First we have to do a collection for a presentation we ain't even invited to . . .

TIMOTHY   You're invited now . . .   5

DAVE   What – as a barman – fixing gin and tonics for our poxy senior management and their wives so's they can have a jolly fine evening at our expense? More ice please young man. Don't you work here as

the lift attendant or something? Very nice little turn out wouldn't
you say? Cheers. I'd rather be a store detective for War on Want   10
sometimes, I tell you.

TIMOTHY   At least you'll be there. None of the other clerks will be.

DEBBIE   It wasn't exactly RSVP with gold lettering though, was it? Not
a hint of you are cordially invited, Mr Gulley requests the pleasure
of your company. Wasn't even would you, could you, please, I'd be   15
grateful. No nothing like that. Quick visit five o'clock last night to
inform us that he wants us to wait on them hand and foot. Only his
euphemism was giving our assistance. Token mention of his appreciation.

TIMOTHY   And a not so token mention that we'd be getting paid for it.   20

DEBBIE   Ever heard of that old-fashioned cliché called the principle of
the thing.

DAVE   It ain't even time and a half.

JOE   I need all the money I can get hold of at the moment. Sandra
says that for the honeymoon she wants to go to Tenerife. And the   25
reception's going to be a four course sit-down with wine included,
followed by a group – spot prizes, special requests and me and
Sandra out on the floor for the first dance. [*Pause.*] They might give
us a tip or something. Like when they have a whip-round for the
coach driver.   30

DAVE   What coach driver?

JOE   Well, generally like. On the way back from wherever you've been.
After the singing.

DAVE   Singing?

JOE   Yeah. *When the Saints Go Marching In.* [*Pause.*] All together.   35
[*Pause.*] Might be like that next week.

DAVE   Oh yeah – I can just see it now. We'll all get together in a big
circle at the end of the evening and do the hokey-kokey.

   Pause.

We don't want tipping – we want our self-respect.

DEBBIE   Won't get much of that when you're having to ask some old   40
berk's wife if she'd like a cherry in her advocaat or coleslaw with her
chicken leg.

TIMOTHY   What are you going to do then – stop watering the office
plants in protest, set fire to the blotting paper and call it industrial
espionage or write a letter of complaint to the staff magazine?   45
Maybe you'll get some placards and march up and down outside
Lawrence's office.

DAVE   [*going deliberately over the top to compete with* TIMOTHY *and hopefully bait him.*]   Yeah, we're going on a go-slow; black the work, withdraw our good-will, picket the stationery cupboard and the executive bog, stand by our entitlements. We're not going to stand for it. In other words, Tim old fruit, we're going to say no. In big letters. Is that simple enough for you? 50

TIMOTHY   I'll hold your coat. [*Pause.*] If one isn't there next week, one is invisible. Not sensible at all. Getting noticed is. Very. 55

DEBBIE   Like a pet dog gets noticed.

TIMOTHY   Pet dogs get fed. Stray ones get put down.

DAVE   Timothy – don't be a bottle job, a wash out, a wally. Don't be the vulture's pickings, the dog's dinner. Know your rights. Don't let your rights go out of the window for the sake of a pat on the head. 60 Dignity. Solidarity. Victory. Stand up and speak out.

> LAWRENCE *has appeared at the door unnoticed at the end of* DAVE's *speech.*

LAWRENCE   Stirring stuff David. When's the battle taking place? Agincourt?

DAVE   I . . . er . . . I was just giving Tim a bit of advice Mr Lawrence – useful tips when buying your Christmas turkey. 65

LAWRENCE   Really. I've just brought this down for next week. [*It is a bar steward's white jacket.*] Could only get hold of one for the time being. I don't know which one of you it'll fit. But you'll be properly kitted out in the end. Don't worry about that.

TIMOTHY   Dave – I don't know if it's slipped your sieve-like mind at all – but didn't you have a few queries about next week. 70

> *Pause.*

LAWRENCE   I'm all ears, as Prince Charles would say.

DAVE   Well . . . the presentation in the evening . . . the function . . . you want us . . . me to work behind the bar . . . serving.

LAWRENCE   I still do. An expert on drink such as yourself is going to be indispensable. 75

DAVE   And Debbie supervising the buffet.

LAWRENCE   A running cold buffet of cooked hams, chicken breast, silverside, home made quiche, various salad mixes, even one with walnuts in it, chicken liver paté, garlic paté, a full selection of cheeses, smoked salmon – Canadian – canapes, potted shrimps, avocado prawn, smoked mackerel, trout, cheese dip, fresh cream gateaux and the perennial sausage rolls. Lot of lovely dishes and I'm sure you'll be the loveliest, Debbie. [*Pause.*] You'll be free to take home with you whatever's left. 80

DAVE   I think, you see . . . 85

89

LAWRENCE [*interrupting.*]   Not getting butterflies or cement mixers or whatever are you? There aren't many that I could trust enough to put on the front line so to speak. I'm sure you'll do justice to the occasion. I know you will. And as far as the etiquette business   90
goes . . .

DAVE   Something else . . . I wanted to talk about, Mr Lawrence. Me and Debbie . . . I don't know about Joe . . . was thinking, not just thinking, saying as well . . . didn't think it was . . . the idea of doing . . . didn't seem what we would have decided . . . for us, I mean our-   95
selves . . . on our own, of our own accord . . . the presentation . . . in the evening . . . agreeing . . .

LAWRENCE   I'm afraid you're making about as much sense as a drunken polar bear.

DAVE   Our job . . . working here . . . it's different . . . that's all we do   100
. . . supposed to . . . normally. What we've been asked that night . . . not the same as what's normal . . . supposed to be working here . . . not the same.

LAWRENCE   You've got a bogey on the side of your nose, David.

   TIMOTHY *laughs.*

LAWRENCE   Only joking. Now what was all that again – you must   105
think I'm terribly slow on the uptake, I think my ears might be full of wax. [*Proffering the side of his head to* DAVID.] Can you see anything? And I hope you're not going to say you can see out through to the other side. Either I'm not listening or you're not communi-
cating. Which d'you think?   110

DAVE   What I meant to say Mr Lawrence . . . about what you want . . .

DEBBIE   We don't want to work as waiters and waitresses next Thursday. We don't think it's fair.

TIMOTHY   Don't include me in that.   115

   Pause.

LAWRENCE   Looks like . . . we've got an insurrection. A mutiny on board. Am I the one you've decided to make walk the plank or what?

   Pause – no response.

Bone of contention seems to concern your appreciation of the con-
ception of what's fair – that right?

DEBBIE   Wouldn't it be possible for you to get someone else to do it Mr   120
Lawrence?

LAWRENCE   More waiters and waitresses you mean? [*Pause.*] On the

registers of numerous employment agencies – experienced, efficient, trained, professional and eminently suitable. But I wanted something much more than that, you see. I thought there was a better   125
way, I really did. To my mind there's a very large distinction between yourselves and the waiters and waitresses you thought you were going to be next Thursday. For a start, you were asked for, wanted – very much so. Because I knew you wouldn't let me down, I knew you'd be a credit to me the department and yourselves. It was a vote   130
of confidence with the best will in the world – not a case of who can we rope in. And that's important for me to make you understand that your presence there is going to be more than just a functional one. If you thought you were just being asked to turn up to pass the peanuts and pour the gin, then I'd be very disappointed in your esti-   135
mation of me and what I'm about. It wouldn't be fair, to use your word.

DEBBIE   What else will we be there for then, Mr Lawrence?

LAWRENCE   Well, on a practical level of course you would be helping to make the evening a success, as you help to make the firm a suc-   140
cess, by working here. I don't normally go in for platitudes, but you are part of a team here, albeit junior members of that team. So wouldn't it be nice if that sense of being part of the firm, of the team, could be reflected in your helping to muck in on Thursday? A symbol of the kind of spirit we try to engender here of people working   145
together, for each other. Next week will be a celebration of twenty-
five years of that spirit. Your refusing to co-operate would sour it. An extra-curricular contribution to Gulley and Co, rather than your normal nine to five one. And I think Mr Gulley is entitled to some small measure of appreciation. After all, he does pay our wages.   150
[*Pause.*] Of course no one is holding a gun to your head or threat-
ening you with thirty lashes for insubordination. This is England, 1982. But probationary reports and promotion markings don't write themselves you know. Attitude – that's the thing.

DEBBIE   We're not trying to sabotage the evening Mr Lawrence or   155
insult Mr Gulley. I thought the collection would have proved that.

LAWRENCE   But I suppose it just goes against your religious beliefs to have anything to do with the firm after five o'clock, to be helpful and approachable only when it says so in your contract of employment.   160

TIMOTHY   I'm quite looking forward to it myself. I won't be washing my hair that night or watching *Crossroads*.

DEBBIE   We won't be there on an equal basis will we?

LAWRENCE   So what's new – you're not here on an equal basis five

days a week. Anyway. I thought I'd explained that aspect of it just 165
now. When you go into a shop – do you think the person giving you
your newspaper or mascara or box of tampons or whatever is some
form of inferior species? Of course you don't – unless your sensibil-
ities are warped. [*Pause.*] OK – so you're not being asked to indulge
in dry sherries and the joys of social intercourse but neither are you 170
going to be treated like Millwall supporters with syphilis.

TIMOTHY   Sweating in the engine room as opposed to standing on the
deck.

DEBBIE   The point is though Mr Lawrence – we'll just be there to help
other people enjoy themselves and clear up after 'em when they've 175
finished. There'll be no celebration of the firm's anniversary for us –
not a proper one anyway. Being an integral part of the spirit of the
whole occasion. I mean, it sounds very nice – but it's hard for us,
me anyway – to appreciate. It seems a bit like that fairy story about
admiring the king's new clothes. You know the one where he ain't 180
wearing nothing at all.

JOE   Danny Kaye sung a song about it.

DEBBIE   You see, I always thought that joining in meant . . . well, what
it sounds like . . . joining in.

LAWRENCE   Well, I don't think we need to make a philosophical issue 185
out of it – or create a maze of excuses. The question remains – either
you want to be constructive or you don't. Abuse my trust or vindi-
cate it. [*Pause.*] You're being very silent David – seen your reservations put into legitimate perspective now have you? Yes? No? Don't
know? 190

DAVE   What Debbie said . . . a lot in common with that. Not the
same as not caring though. I think I might be babysitting for me
sister next Thursday. She lives in Ilford. I have to get a 25 from
Stratford.

LAWRENCE   I would really like to go away from here feeling that apart 195
from Tim there was some kind of commitment and interest that
went beyond salary – which I think is due for review next month, is
it not? [*Pause.*] What about Joe – prepared to put yourself out, start
off on the right note and show me that the firm's taken on a
winner? 200

JOE   No, I don't mind actually. Broaden my working experience won't
it and . . . help me develop my office skills . . . like communication
. . . in a social environment. Showing the right attitude – be an asset
like. Only thing is though – I'm a bit accident prone. Last do I went
to I got an olive stuck up me nose. That was just before I opened 205
this bottle of Pomagne – the cork hit this woman right in the eye,

made her false teeth fall out . . . into the coleslaw. I had to leave early. I'm sure I'll be all right next Thursday though.

LAWRENCE   How reassuring. Remember earlier on you were talking about what's fair. Would your definition of fair include the use of the   210 democratic process, abiding by the majority decision for the good of the community and all that. Would it?

DAVE *and* DEBBIE *both shrug, nod.*

Funny you should say that because if I've got my sums right and a fair and democratic vote took place, it would be two against two with me having the casting vote and consequently next Thursday   215 would be graced by both your presences.

DEBBIE   We also believe in freedom of choice Mr Lawrence.

LAWRENCE   Let me put your freedom of choice into perspective. I was talking about this being England, 1982. Last week, personnel had 250 applications for two vacant clerical posts they advertised.   220 Amazing isn't it? Steady, decent jobs are rare things today. You're in very fortunate positions, you're what's known as the lucky ones. Plenty of people anxious to be where you are now, to push you off the perch. 250. 250 applications for two posts. Employers have freedom of choice at the moment – bags of it. [*Pause.*] Having a job   225 today, especially for young people – well, it's like having a life raft to hold onto in a very cold, hostile sea – something to cling onto desperately. Only fools would want to do something that might jeopardise their tenuous grip on the life raft, see their fingers being prised away and find themselves stranded in an ocean of nothing. An   230 ocean of unemployment. And there'd be nowhere else to go believe me – not even for bright young sparks like yourselves. Sobering thought isn't it? And of course that makes it so much more crucial that you please your employers. You'd do well to bear that in mind and start looking over your shoulders. Let me know when you've   235 seen the light. Cheers.

He goes out.

DAVE   Happy birthday Gulley & Co.

TIMOTHY [*who has put on the bar steward's jacket*]   How's it look?

DEBBIE   Looks like trouble.

Understanding the text

1   Compare Timothy and Dave's attitude to the extra work they are being asked to do. Look, for example, at comments like:

TIMOTHY   If one isn't there next week, one is invisible. Not sensible at all. Getting noticed is.
DAVE   Don't let your rights go out of the window for the sake of a pat on the head.

Divide a sheet of paper into two and list as many comments like those above as you can in the appropriate columns.

2   What difference is there between the way Dave talks to Timothy and the way he talks to Lawrence? What does this tell us about Dave?

3   Lawrence puts a number of reasons forward for wanting the young staff to help at the party. Try to list all the reasons he gives. Which do you think would be the most important to him personally?

4   This is a very 'verbal' scene. People say a great deal, but after Lawrence comes in much of what they say seems careful and guarded as if they're not really saying what they mean. Try to summarise the attitudes of each of the characters and say who you think has most to gain and most to lose through the way they deal with the situation.

Producing the scene

1   Design a set which would reflect the boring nature of the job the young staff are doing in the basement. What furniture and colour scheme would you use? Try to make your design and notes as detailed as possible.

2   How could the actors use their voices to reflect the different backgrounds and aspirations of the characters they are playing? Imagine you are auditioning for one of the parts. Choose no more than six lines and rehearse them on your own, developing what you consider to be an appropriate accent and tone of voice. Find another member of the group who has chosen the same character and compare your methods and results.

3   Look at the moment when Lawrence first enters. Act out this entrance and see if you can achieve a laugh from the audience by the way you position the characters at this moment and the timing of the actual entrance.

4   What advice would you give to the actors as to how they should react to the entrance of Lawrence in order to show both their feelings towards him and each other? Act out the entrance scene again and freeze after Lawrence's line, 'When's the battle taking place?' Allow each character to speak aloud one thought about Dave, Debbie and Lawrence. Replay the scene a third time and

see if it is possible to 'choreograph' the facial expressions and glances in order to make these secret thoughts obvious to an audience.

5   Look at Debbie's last line and, in groups of four, pose for a still photograph. How could the positioning indicate what might happen next? Experiment with changing people's positions so that they suggest various alternatives.

6   Discuss what attitude you think the audience should have towards both the characters and the forthcoming party at the end of this scene. What do you personally feel about the situation that the young people have been put in here?

Further development

1   In groups of three invent a situation in which A wants B to do something. B is openly opposed to this but C tries to keep the peace.

2   Lawrence tells the others that the firm had received 250 applications for two posts. In pairs, improvise an interview in which Lawrence, or a character like him, is interviewing someone like Dave who doesn't really like the look of the job but needs it.

3   Lawrence tries to persuade the others to 'toe the line' but underlying his persuasion are veiled threats. In pairs, improvise a scene in which someone is persuading someone else to do something, but the more they resist, the more the persuasion becomes menacing.

4   Act out the scene at the presentation party. Does Dave take his revenge? If so, how? (Of course, if you want to know what really happens you'll have to read the whole play!)

5   'You're in very fortunate positions, you're what's known as the lucky ones.' Do you think they are lucky? What do you think Dave, Debbie, Joe and Timothy are sacrificing in order to keep their jobs? People on strike often face a dilemma – do they preserve their 'self-respect' at the risk of being 'fools' who 'jeopardise their tenuous grip on the life raft', or should they 'get noticed' in the way Timothy suggests? Write or prepare an improvisation telling a story which explores such a dilemma. (Your improvisation does not necessarily have to be about a strike.)

6   *The Lucky Ones* is quite unusual in that it deals with some of the problems faced by young people. What other difficult situations do young people face which you think might make a good subject for a play? List the possibilities and try to tie a number of them together in a written or improvised story.

7   As a whole class create an instant 'waxwork' representation called 'Britain Today'. Your class teacher could select small numbers of you in turn to leave the display and look at what the others are doing. What themes seem to be most strongly represented? Is this a reflection of life in your area or of how you perceive life in Britain today generally?

VINEGAR TOM

by Caryl Churchill

CAST (in order of appearance)

BELLRINGER

MARGERY

JACK

PACKER

GOODY

JOAN

SUSAN

ALICE

BETTY

ELLEN

10 speaking parts. Doubling possible.

On the surface one might say that *Vinegar Tom* was a play about witches. A closer look might suggest that it's about how women are accused of being witches. Go deeper again and one might see that the play also makes statements about *why* women are accused of being witches. In many ways *Vinegar Tom* is a historical play, inspired by the accounts of the witch-hunts of the seventeenth century. In the turmoil just after the Civil War, new ways of thinking were struggling for general acceptance. The Parliamentarians (Roundheads) tended to apply the teachings of the Bible in strict and very male-orientated ways. Caryl Churchill's play takes place in a world in which the puritanical Roundheads are trying to create a more modern and 'professional' society. The old-fashioned practices of 'cunning women' with their folk medicine and herbal remedies were seen as a threat to progress. Caryl Churchill notes that 'the women accused of witchcraft were often those on the edges of society: old, poor, single, sexually unconventional'. The qualities of such women – notably their skill with herbs, their knowledge of human nature and ability to give good advice – had been valued in their own communities. But then, as always, unconventional people were seen as a threat by those in authority. Accusing a woman of being a witch was a way of punishing her for not being 'normal', and also a warning to other women to fall into line or suffer the consequences.

Caryl Churchill has written a play not so much about witchcraft as about how women saw themselves and how changes in society affected that. There is a clear and strong undercurrent in the play suggesting that society today is still in the grip of many of the attitudes of that time. The story follows the fortunes of Alice and her mother, Joan. Alice is pursued by a frustrated married man, Jack. When she refuses to go to bed with him he calls her a witch. In the meantime his equally bitter wife, Margery, takes out her frustration on Joan by accusing her also of being a witch. The arrival of a witchfinder and his assistant in the village gives those who want it the chance to 'get even' and settle their petty grievances in a gruesome way.

The style of the play

Vinegar Tom is a blunt and cold play. The audience are shown scenes depicting how the witch-hunt affects the local people. The story of Alice and Joan is told in a straightforward, chronological way. The play is interspersed with songs which seem to relate the events of 300 years ago to the present day.

The extract

Jack and his wife, Margery, both have personal reasons for wanting vengeance on Alice and Joan. Alice's friend Susan has just lost a baby and needs to blame someone. A local cunning woman, Ellen, is another easy target for the witchfinder, Packer, and his sadistic assistant, Goody Haskins, who have just arrived in the village. The other characters in the extract are Betty – another friend of Alice's – and a bellringer who announces the arrival of the witchfinder.

Scene fourteen

BELLRINGER   Whereas if anyone has any complaint against any woman for a witch, let them go to the townhall and lay their complaint. For a man is in town that is a famous finder of witches and has had above thirty hanged in the country round and he will discover if they are or no. Whereas if anyone has any complaint against any   5
woman for a witch, let them go . . .
MARGERY   Stopped the butter.
JACK   Killed the calves.

MARGERY   Struck me in the head.

JACK   Lamed my hand.   10

MARGERY   Struck me in the stomach.

JACK   Bewitched my organ.

MARGERY   When I boiled my urine she came.

JACK   Blooded her and made my hand well.

MARGERY   Burnt her thatch.   15

JACK   And Susan, her friend, is like possessed screaming and crying
and lay two days without speaking.

MARGERY   Susan's baby turned blue and its limbs twisted and it died.

JACK   Boy threw stones and called them witch, and after he vomited
pins and straw.   20

MARGERY   Big nasty cat she has in her bed and sends it to people's
dairies.

JACK   A rat's her imp.

MARGERY   And the great storm last night brought a tree down in the
lane, who made that out of a clear sky?   25

PACKER   I thank God that he has brought me again where I am
needed. Don't be afraid any more. You have been in great danger
but the devil can never overcome the faithful. For God in his mercy
has called me and shown me a wonderful way of finding out witches,
which is finding the place on the body of the witch made insensi-   30
tive to pain by the devil. So that if you prick that place with a pin
no blood comes out and the witch feels nothing at all.

> PACKER *and* GOODY *take* JOAN, *and* GOODY *holds her, while* PACKER
> *pulls up her skirts and pricks her legs.* JOAN *curses and screams*
> *throughout.* PACKER *and* GOODY *abuse her: a short sharp moment of*
> *great noise and confusion.*

GOODY   Hold still you old witch. Devil not help you now, no good
calling him. Strong for your age, that's the devil's strength in her,
see. Hold still, you stinking old strumpet . . .   35

PACKER   Hold your noise, witch, how can we tell what we're doing?
Ah, ah, there's for you devil, there's blood, and there's blood,
where's your spot, we'll find you out Satan . . .

JOAN   Damn you to hell, oh Christ help me! Ah, ah, you're hurting, let
go, damn you, oh sweet God, oh you devils, oh devil take you . . .   40

PACKER   There, there, no blood here, Goody Haskins. Here's her spot.
Hardly a speck here.

GOODY   How she cries the old liar, pretending it hurts her.

PACKER   There's one for hanging, stand aside there. We've others to
attend to. Next please, Goody.   45

GOODY *takes* ALICE. PACKER *helps, and her skirts are thrown over her head while he pricks her. She tries not to cry out.*

GOODY Why so much blood?

PACKER The devil's cunning here.

GOODY She's not crying much, she can't feel it.

PACKER Have I the spot though? Which is the spot? There. There. There. No, I haven't the spot. Oh, it's tiring work. Set this one aside. Maybe there's others will speak against her and let us know more clearly what she is.   50

ALICE *is stood aside.*

PACKER If anyone here knows anything more of this woman why she might be a witch, I charge them in God's name to speak out, or the guilt of filthy witchcraft will be on you for concealing it.   55

SUSAN I know something of her.

PACKER Don't be shy then girl, speak out.

ALICE Susan, what you doing? Don't speak against me.

SUSAN Don't let her at me.

ALICE You'll have me hanged.   60

SUSAN *starts to shriek hysterically.*

GOODY Look, she's bewitched.

MARGERY It's Alice did it to her.

ALICE Susan, stop.

SUSAN Alice. Alice. Alice.

PACKER Take the witch out and the girl may be quiet.   65

GOODY *takes* ALICE *off.* SUSAN *stops.*

MARGERY See that.

JACK Praise God I escaped such danger.

SUSAN She met with the devil, she told me, like a man in black she met him in the night and did uncleanness with him, and ever after she was not herself but wanted to be with the devil again. She took me to a cunning woman and they made me take a foul potion to destroy the baby in my womb and it was destroyed. And the cunning woman said she would teach Alice her wicked magic, and she'd have powers and not everyone could learn that, but Alice could because she's a witch, and the cunning woman gave her something to call the devil, and she tried to call him, and she made a puppet, and stuck pins in, and tried to make me believe that was the devil, but that was my baby girl, and next day she was sick and her face   70   75 blue and limbs all twisted up and she died. And I don't want to see her. 80

PACKER   These cunning women are worst of all. Everyone hates witches who do harm but good witches they go to for help and come into the devil's power without knowing it. The infection will spread through the whole country if we don't stop it. Yes, all witches deserve death, and the good witch even more than the bad one. Oh 85 God, do not let your kingdom be overrun by the devil. And you, girl, you went to this good witch, and you destroyed the child in your womb by witchcraft, which is a grievous offence. And you were there when this puppet was stuck with pins, and consented to the death of your own baby daughter? 90

SUSAN   No, I didn't. I didn't consent. I never wished her harm. Oh if I was angry sometimes or cursed her for crying, I never meant it. I'd take it back if I could have her back. I never meant to harm her.

PACKER   You can't take your curses back, you cursed her to death. That's two of your children you killed. And what other harm have 95 you done? Don't look amazed, you'll speak soon enough. We'll prick you as you pricked your babies.

Scene fifteen

GOODY *takes* SUSAN *and* PACKER *pulls up her skirt.*

GOODY   There's no man finds more witches than Henry Packer. He can tell by their look, he says, but of course he has more ways than that. He's read all the books and he's travelled. He says the reason 100 there's so much witchcraft in England is England is too soft with its witches, for in Europe and Scotland they are hanged and burned and if they are not penitent they are burnt alive, but in England they are only hanged. And the ways of discovering witches are not so good here, for in other countries they have thumbscrews and racks 105 and the bootikens which is said to be the worst pain in the world, for it fits tight over the legs from ankle to knee and is driven tighter and tighter till the legs are crushed as small as might be and the blood and marrow spout out and the bones crushed and the legs made unserviceable forever. And very few continue their lies and 110 denials then. In England we haven't got such thorough ways, our ways are slower but they get the truth in the end when a fine skil-ful man like Henry Packer is onto them. He's well worth the twenty shillings a time, and I get the same, which is very good of him to insist on and well worth it though some folk complain and say, 115 'what, the price of a cow, just to have a witch hanged?' But I say to

them think of the expense a witch is to you in the damage she does
to property, such as a cow killed one or two pounds, a horse maybe
four pounds, besides all the pigs and sheep at a few shillings a time,
and chickens at sixpence all adds up. For two pounds and our   120
expenses at the inn, you have all that saving, besides knowing you're
free of the threat of sudden illness and death. Yes, it's interesting
work being a searcher and nice to do good at the same time as earn-
ing a living. Better than staying home a widow. I'd end up like the
old women you see, soft in the head and full of spite with their mutt-   125
ering and spells. I keep healthy keeping the country healthy. It's an
honour to work with a great professional.

Scene sixteen

BETTY   I'm frightened to come any more. They'll say I'm a witch.

ELLEN   Are they saying I'm a witch?

BETTY   They say because I screamed that was the devil in me. And   130
when I ran out of the house they say where was I going if not to
meet other witches. And some know I come to see you.

ELLEN   Nobody's said it yet to my face.

BETTY   But the doctor says he'll save me. He says I'm not a witch, he
says I'm ill. He says I'm his patient so I can't be a witch. He says he's   135
making me better. I hope I can be better.

ELLEN   You get married, Betty, that's safest.

BETTY   But I want to be left alone. You know I do.

ELLEN   Left alone for what? To be like me? There's no doctor going to
save me from being called a witch. Your best chance of being left   140
alone is marry a rich man, because it's part of his honour to have a
wife who does nothing. He has his big house and rose garden and
trout stream, he just needs a fine lady to make it complete and you
can be that. You can sing and sit on the lawn and change your dresses
and order the dinner. That's the best you can do. What would you   145
rather? Marry a poor man and work all day? Or go on as you're going,
go on strange? That's not safe. Plenty of girls feel like you've been
feeling, just for a bit. But you're not one to go on with it.

BETTY   If it's true there's witches, maybe I've been bewitched. If the
witches are stopped maybe I'll get well.   150

ELLEN   You'll get well, my dear, and you'll get married, and you'll tell
your children about the witches.

BETTY   What's going to happen? Will you be all right?

ELLEN   You go home now. You don't want them finding you here.

BETTY *goes.*

I could ask to be swum. They think the water won't keep a witch in,   155
for Christ's baptism sake, so if a woman floats she's a witch. And if
she sinks they have to let her go. I could sink. Any fool can sink.
It's how to sink without drowning. It's whether they get you out. No,
why should I ask to be half drowned? I've done nothing. I'll explain
to them what I do. It's healing, not harm. There's no devil in it. If I   160
keep calm and explain it, they can't hurt me.

If you float

If you float you're a witch
If you scream you're a witch
If you sink, then you're dead anyway.   165
If you cure you're a witch
Or impure you're a witch
Whatever you do, you must pay.
Fingers are pointed, a knock at the door,
You may be a mother, a child or a whore.   170
If you complain you're a witch
Or you're lame you're a witch
Any marks or deviations count for more.
Got bit tits you're a witch
Fall to bits you're a witch   175
He likes them young, concupiscent and poor.
Fingers are pointed, a knock on the door,
They're coming to get you, do you know what for?
So don't drop a stitch
My poor little bitch   180
If you're making a spell
Do it well.
Deny it you're bad
Admit it you're mad
Say nothing at all   185
They'll damn you to hell.

Understanding the text

1   Read through the script and make a note, as you do so, of all the comments
or remarks that might be used as evidence that someone is a witch. Look carefully at your list and divide them into two sets, those that appear to be based on
fact, and those that seem to be based on superstition.

2 List the various methods of discovering witches mentioned in the extract. What do you think the author's intention is in including these descriptions?

3 What reasons does Goody Haskins give for working for Packer? Consider her comment: 'Better than staying at home a widow. I'd end up like the old women you see, soft in the head and full of spite with their muttering and spells.' In what way does this affect your opinion of her and what she is doing?

4 Why do you think Ellen, the local 'cunning woman', says, 'There's no doctor going to save me from being called a witch'? Why do you think getting married will help save Betty from being accused?

5 Scene Fourteen seems to consist of a number of different sections, as if time has been condensed and the audience are only being shown the 'edited highlights' of the events rather than one whole scene that actually took place. Make a note of where each block of time seems to end and a new one begins.

Producing the scene

1 No stage directions are given as to where each scene might be taking place. Suggest:
- a possible setting for each scene
- a way of representing that place simply
- an appropriate lighting state for each scene.

2 With so many quick changes of scene it might be easier to act the play on a very bare stage. List three advantages and three possible disadvantages of this method.

3 In the opening section of this extract, where Jack and Margery are giving details of what they think Joan has done to them, the lines are very short, blunt and quite rhythmical. Try to rehearse the lines 'Stopped the butter' to 'Burnt her thatch', emphasising a rhythm. In groups of four or five make up a few more accusations in the same style and experiment with ways of speaking them to a set beat. Try whispering them and see if this might also create a good effect.

4 Make a set of 'director's notes' which could be used to advise the actress playing Goody Haskins when she is tackling her long speech in Scene Fifteen. Make a note of anything that she ought to do, or anything that is going on in the background. Remember, any action should add to rather than distract from what she is saying.

5 An alternative to singing 'If You Float' would be to use 'choral speech'. In groups of at least four divide the lines up between different speakers, for example:
1 If you float you're a witch
2 If you scream you're a witch
3 If you sink
4 then you're dead anyway

and so on. Some lines could be said by two or more people together and some perhaps by the whole group. The point is to capture the rhythm of the writing while emphasising the point it is trying to make.

6   Consider the way you have decided to deliver the lines of 'If You Float'. Then consider how you might position or move the chorus around to make a visual as well as an aural impact on the audience.

Further development

1   Packer seems to have already decided who is guilty. Improvise a scene in which one person is trying to defend herself against one or more others who have already decided on her guilt.

2   In the extract Alice is betrayed by her friend Susan, who then tries to deny that she meant what she said. Imagine a scene in which the two characters meet again in a cell. How would Susan explain her action and what would Alice's reaction be?

3   What sort of circumstances might lead someone to betray a close friend? Make up a story in which someone comes under pressure in some way which results in a betrayal. You might be able to think of actual historical events where you can imagine this happening.

4   This extract presents a number of assumptions about women who behave in ways which don't fit in with society's expectations. Is there anything that girls do today which causes people to assume something about them? What sort of assumptions, for example, would a girl who wanted to be a lorry driver have to face up to? Write or improvise a scene in which a woman has to face up to such assumptions. (If you are interested in this area you may enjoy Clare Luckham's play *Trafford Tanzi*.)

5   Imagine that the tide of history turned in such a way as to place women in positions of power while Packer was still alive. Set up a courtroom scene in which Packer is tried for crimes against women. What assumptions might be made about the type of man he is and why he was doing what he was doing? Who would give evidence against him and how could he be defended?

6   Actually staging an execution could create a number of problems. It would be important not to do it in such a way that the audience either laughed or felt sick – this would take their attention away from the unfairness of what was being done. Experiment with ways of staging such a scene which would successfully make the audience feel anger at the injustice.

7   Think of a group of people from any period of history (including the present day) who are seen as easy targets for persecution, in the same way as women are in *Vinegar Tom*. Look carefully at the language of 'If You Float' and use the style as the basis for a piece of choral speech of your own which explores the unfairness of how certain groups of people are treated.

BLACK COMEDY

by Peter Shaffer

CAST (in order of appearance)

BRINDSLEY

CAROL

SCHUPPANZIGH

COLONEL

HAROLD

CLEA

6 speaking parts.

Farce has existed as a form of comedy since the ancient Greeks first started to write and perform theatre. In a farce, the audience is invited to laugh at characters as they find themselves in increasingly complicated situations which inevitably lead them to some kind of humiliation. The old saying that 'the bigger they are, the harder they fall' is a sort of rule in this type of comedy. In farce, the characters are to some extent the authors of their own downfall; the bigger their ego, the more pompous they are or the more they try to pretend to be something they are not, then the more likely they are to suffer indignity and exposure. Farce relies on exaggeration and caricature: we can't wholly believe the characters are real and the situations they find themselves in are similarly quite unbelievable. Nevertheless, farce invites us to recognise our own faults and the fact that life can be totally unpredictable. However, at the end of a good farce all of the characters seem to survive without too serious a loss of face and end up, like the audience, a little wiser about themselves and the dangers of imagining that we are in complete control of our lives.

Black Comedy is a good example of a typical English farce. The characters are middle-class stereotypes. They seem self-confident, polite and secure in the belief that nothing terrible is ever likely to happen to them. The comedy comes, of course, when something extraordinary does happen. Peter Shaffer takes the title for his play from a form of comedy closely related to farce. In 'black comedy' the audience is made to laugh at things which are normally considered tragic, such as death and cruelty, but Shaffer takes the term literally. The play is set in the London apartment of a young sculptor, Brindsley Miller. In order to impress his fiancée's father, Colonel Melkett, Brindsley has borrowed a number of expensive pieces of furniture and ornaments from his neighbour's flat. He has also arranged for a rich and famous art collector to visit. Things start to go horribly wrong, though, when a fuse blows and throws the apartment into total darkness. Not only does the prissy neighbour, Harold Gorringe, turn up unexpectedly which forces Brindsley to try and replace all of his belongings in the dark, but his ex-girlfriend also arrives, intent on ruining his engagement. The genius of the play is in the way light and dark are swapped so that what is darkness to the characters is visible to the audience and vice versa. In this way, the play is a wonderful example of dramatic irony in that the audience sees what the characters themselves cannot.

The style of the play

Farce needs to move quickly. In *Black Comedy* the initial problem of all the lights going out accelerates into a situation which becomes more and more difficult for Brindsley. As he tries to impress the Colonel, replace Harold's furniture and keep his ex-girlfriend Clea out of the way he becomes like a manic juggler as the other characters throw him more and more balls to try and keep off the ground. The greatest danger to Brindsley is that the lights will come back on before he is ready for them; every time someone strikes a match or shines a torch he is in danger of being found out. The way the play is lit is crucial to the comedy and demands split-second timing between the actors and the lighting technician.

The extract

This extract comes from near the end of the play. A humble yet cultured electrician has turned up to mend the blown fuse. His German accent leads Brindsley and the others to mistake him for the millionaire art collector that has been invited to review Brindsley's work, but their mistake is quickly discovered. Just as Brindsley seems to have successfully dealt with this situation, though, Clea takes advantage of the darkness to cause more trouble for him.

BRINDSLEY   Oh, Christ!
CAROL   What!
BRINDSLEY [*sotto voce*]   *The sofa . . .!* I'd forgotten about *the sofa*! Let's get that bloody torch away from him!

106

SCHUPPANZIGH [*shining his torch at them*]   Excuse me, but I am pressed   5
　for time.
BRINDSLEY   Of course – of course . . . [*He throws himself on the sofa,
　spreading wide his arms to conceal it.*]
SCHUPPANZIGH [*he spies the sculpture in iron*]   Oh Gott in Himmel . . .!
　Is that one of yours?   10
BRINDSLEY   Yes.
SCHUPPANZIGH   It's amazing. Absolutely phantastisch!
BRINDSLEY   You really think so?
SCHUPPANZIGH   But definitely. I see at once what it represents.
COLONEL   You do?   15
SCHUPPANZIGH   Oh, no question. The two needles of man's unrest.
　Self-love and self-hate, leading to the same point! [*He swings the
　torch back to* BRINDSLEY. BRINDSLEY *again covers the sofa with his body.*]
　I'm right, aren't I?
BRINDSLEY   Absolutely . . . It's easy to see you're an expert, sir!   20
SCHUPPANZIGH   Aber nein, nein!
BRINDSLEY   May I suggest an experiment? I would love you to feel it
　in the dark!
SCHUPPANZIGH   The dark?
BRINDSLEY   Yes, I actually made that piece to be felt, not seen. I call   25
　it my theory of Factual Tactility. If it doesn't stab you to the quick,
　it's not Art. [*To* CAROL.] Darling, why don't you relieve our distin-
　guished guest of his torch, and he can try this for himself?

　　SCHUPPANZIGH *surrenders his torch to* CAROL, *who turns it off. The
　　stage brightens. Immediately,* BRINDSLEY *rises from the sofa.*

CAROL   Oh yes. Of course . . .
BRINDSLEY   Now stretch out your arms and feel it all over, sir. With   30
　passion – that's the trick. Total *commitment*!
SCHUPPANZIGH   Ach – wunderbar! Impaled here in the dark, one can
　feel the vital thrust of the argument. The anguish of our times! It
　has real moral force! I feel the passionate embrace of similarities to
　create an orgasm of opposites.   35
CAROL   Oh, how super!
SCHUPPANZIGH   You should charge immense sums for work like this,
　Mr Miller. This one, for example, how much is this?
BRINDSLEY   Fifty –
CAROL   Five hundred guineas!   40
SCHUPPANZIGH   Ach so! [*He pauses.*] Well . . .
HAROLD   Would you like it then?
SCHUPPANZIGH   Very much.

COLONEL [*amazed*]   For five hundred guineas?
SCHUPPANZIGH   Certainly – if I had it!   45

    All laugh fawningly.

HAROLD   You mean you've gone broke?
SCHUPPANZIGH   No. I mean I never had it.
COLONEL   Now look, sir, I know millionaires are supposed to be eccentric . . .
CAROL   Daddy, ssh!   50
SCHUPPANZIGH   Millionaires? Who do you think I am?
COLONEL   Dammit, man! You must know who you are!
CAROL   Mr Bamberger, is this some kind of joke you like to play?
SCHUPPANZIGH   Excuse me. That is not my name.
BRINDSLEY   It isn't?   55
SCHUPPANZIGH   No. My name is Schuppanzigh. Franz Immanuel Schuppanzigh. Born in Weimar, 1905. Student of philosophy at Heidelberg, 1934. Refugee to this country, 1938. Regular employment ever since – with the London Electricity Board!
CAROL   Electricity!   60
BRINDSLEY   You mean you're not – ?
HAROLD   Of course he's not!
SCHUPPANZIGH   But who did you imagine I was?
HAROLD [*furiously*]   How dare you? [*He snatches the electrician's torch from* CAROL *and turns it on.*]   65

    The stage darkens.

SCHUPPANZIGH [*retreating before him*]   Please?
HAROLD   Of all the nerve, coming in here, giving us a lecture about orgasms, and all the time you're simply here to mend a fuse!
COLONEL   I agree with you, sir. It's monstrous!
SCHUPPANZIGH [*bewildered*]   It is?   70

    The COLONEL *snatches the torch and shines it pitilessly in the man's face.*

COLONEL   You come in here, a public servant, pretending to be deaf, and proceed to harangue your employers, unasked and uninvited.
SCHUPPANZIGH [*bewildered*]   Excuse me. But I *was* invited.
COLONEL   Don't answer me back. In my day you would have been fired on the spot for impertinence.   75
CAROL   Daddy's absolutely right! Ever since the Beatles, the lower classes think they can behave exactly as they want.
COLONEL [*handing the torch to* BRINDSLEY]   Miller, will you kindly show this feller his work?

BRINDSLEY [*exasperated*]   Why don't you just go into the cellar?   80
SCHUPPANZIGH [*snatching the torch, equally exasperated*]   All right!
   Where is it?
HAROLD [*seizing the torch*]   I'll do it. [*To* SCHUPPANZIGH.] Come on.
   Down you go. Come on, get a move on!
SCHUPPANZIGH   All right! So – farewell!   85

> SCHUPPANZIGH *descends through the trap, taking the torch with him.*

[*Calling up from below.*] I leave the light of Art for the dark of
Science!
HAROLD   Let's have a little less of your lip, shall we? [*He slams the
   trapdoor down irritably after him.*]

> *The lights immediately come up full. There is a long pause. All stand
> about embarrassed. Above, attracted by the noise of the slam* CLEA
> *gets out of bed, still clutching the vodka and toothmug, opens the door,
> and stands at the top of the stairs listening.*

BRINDSLEY   None of this evening is happening.   90
CAROL   Cheer up, darling. In a few minutes everything will be all
   right. Mr Bamberger will arrive in the light – he'll adore your work
   and give you twenty thousand pounds for your whole collection.
BRINDSLEY [*sarcastically*]   Oh, yes!
CAROL   Then we can buy a super little house and live what's laugh-   95
   ingly known as happily ever after. I want to leave this place just as
   soon as we're *married*.

> CLEA *hears this. Her mouth opens wide with astonishment.*

BRINDSLEY [*nervously*]   Shhhh!
CAROL   Why? I don't want to live in a slum for our first couple of years
   – like other newly-weds.   100
BRINDSLEY   Shhh! Shhhh!
CAROL   What's the matter with you?
BRINDSLEY   The gods listen, darling. They've given me a terrible night
   so far. They may do worse.
CAROL [*cooing*]   I know, darling. You've had a filthy evening. Poor   105
   baby. But I'll fight them with you. I don't care a fig for those naughty
   old gods. [*She looks up.*] Do you hear? Not a single little figipoo!

> CLEA *aims at the voice and sends a jet of vodka splashing down over*
> CAROL.

Ahh!!!
BRINDSLEY   What is it?

CAROL It's raining! 110
BRINDSLEY Don't be stupid.
CAROL I'm all wet!
BRINDSLEY How can you be?

CLEA *throws vodka over a wider area.* HAROLD *gets it.*

HAROLD Hey, what's going on?
BRINDSLEY What? 115
COLONEL What are you hollerin' for?

He gets a slug of vodka in the face.

Ahh!
BRINDSLEY [*inspired*] It's a leak – the water mains must have gone now!
HAROLD Oh, good God! 120
BRINDSLEY It must be!

Mischievously, CLEA *raps her bottle loudly on the top stair. There is a terrified silence. All look up. Pause.*

HAROLD Don't say there's someone else here.
BRINDSLEY Good Lord!
COLONEL Who's there?

Silence from above.

Come on! I know you're there! 125

Pause.

BRINDSLEY [*improvising wildly*] I – I bet you it's Mrs Punnet.

CLEA *looks astonished.*

COLONEL Who?
BRINDSLEY [*for* CLEA's *benefit*] Mrs Punnet. My cleaning woman. She comes here every Friday.
CAROL But what would she be doing here *now*? 130
BRINDSLEY I – I've just remembered! I mentioned to her yesterday I was giving a party tonight and she said she'd look in and tidy up the place for me!
COLONEL But dammit man, it's ten o'clock!
HAROLD She can't be that conscientious! Not from what you've told 135 me.
BRINDSLEY Oh, but she is! You haven't met her – you can't *imagine* how devoted she is . . .! One night she turned up at *midnight*, and

told me she couldn't sleep for thinking how dirty the place might
be! 140

COLONEL But when did she come?

BRINDSLEY She probably just slipped in and upstairs without our hearing. She's very discreet. She actually wears special swansdown slippers to keep the noise to the minimum.

COLONEL Well, let's just see if it's her, shall we? 145

BRINDSLEY Oh no, sir – she hates being disturbed!

COLONEL [calling] Mrs Punnet ...! Is that you ...? [Louder.] Mrs
Punnet!!!

Pause.

CLEA [deliberately deciding on an old Cockney voice] 'Allo! Yes?

BRINDSLEY [weakly] It is. Good heavens, Mrs Punnet, what on earth 150
are you doing up there?

CLEA I'm giving your bedroom a bit of a tidy, sir.

BRINDSLEY At this time of night?

The mischief in CLEA *begins to take over.*

CLEA I'm afraid I was delayed, but better late than never, sir, as they
say. I know how you like your bedroom to be nice and inviting when 155
you're giving one of your parties.

COLONEL When did you come, madam?

CLEA Just a few minutes ago, sir. I didn't like to disturb you, so I came
on up 'ere. But I can't seem to find the light. It's as dark as
Newgate's Knocker ... Are you playing one of your kinky games, 160
Mr Miller?

BRINDSLEY No, Mrs Punnet. We've had a fuse. It's all over the house.

CLEA Oh, a fuse! I thought it might be one of your kinky games in
the dark, sir. Perhaps the one with the rubber underclothes and
those little whips. [She starts to come downstairs.] 165

BRINDSLEY [distinctly] It is a fuse, Mrs Punnet. The man is mending it
now. The lights will be on *any minute!*

CLEA Well, that'll be a relief for you, won't it? [She dashes the vodka
accurately in his face, passes him by, and comes into the room.]

BRINDSLEY Yes, of course. Now, why don't you just go on home now? 170
There's nothing you can do here tonight.

CLEA Are you sure of that, sir?

During the following, BRINDSLEY *gropes around the room frantically
to find her, but she eludes him.*

BRINDSLEY Well not with this fuse – it's pointless, isn't it?

CLEA   Oh no, sir! I could clean this place with my eyes shut. And I'd like to – really! I'd hate your guests to see it as it usually is. Bras and panties in the sink – contraceptives on the floor – and marriage-uana seeds simply *everywhere*!   175

> BRINDSLEY *muzzles her with his hand. She bites it hard, and he drops to his knees in silent agony.*

COLONEL   Please watch what you say, madam. You don't know it, but you are in the presence of Mr Miller's fiancée.

CLEA   Fiancée?   180

COLONEL   Yes, and I am her father.

CLEA   Well, I never . . .! Oh, Mr Miller! I'm so 'appy for you . . .! Fiancée! Oh, sir. And you never *told* me!

BRINDSLEY   I was keeping it a surprise.

CLEA   Well, I never! Oh, how lovely . . .! May I kiss you, sir, please?   185

BRINDSLEY [*on his knees*]   Well, yes, yes, of course . . .

> CLEA *gropes for his ear, finds it, and twists it.*

CLEA   Oh, sir, I'm so pleased for you! And for *you*, miss too!

CAROL   Thank you.

CLEA [*to* COLONEL]   And for *you*, sir.

COLONEL   Thank you.   190

CLEA [*wickedly*]   You must be – Miss Clea's father!

COLONEL   Miss Clea? I don't understand.

> *Triumphantly,* CLEA *sticks out her tongue at* BRINDSLEY, *who collapses his length on the floor, face down, in a gesture of total surrender. For him it is the end. The evening can hold no further disasters for him.*

CLEA [*to* CAROL]   Well, I never! So you've got him at last! Well done, Miss Clea! I never thought you would – not after four years . . .

BRINDSLEY   No – no – no – no . . .!   195

CLEA   Forgive me, sir, if I'm speaking out of turn, but you must admit you take a long time proposing. Four years is a long time to be courting one woman.

BRINDSLEY [*weakly*]   Mrs Punnet, *please*!

CAROL   Four years?   200

CLEA   Well, yes, dear. It's been all of that and a bit more, hasn't it? [*In a stage whisper.*] And of course it's just in time really, isn't it? It was getting a bit prominent, your little bun in the oven.

> CAROL *screeches with disgust.* BRINDSLEY *covers his ears.*

Oh, Miss, I don't mean that's why he popped the question. Of course it's not. He's always been stuck on you. He told me so, not one week ago, in this room. [*Sentimentally.*] 'Mrs Punnet,' he says, 'Mrs Punnet, as far as I'm concerned you can keep the rest of them – Miss Clea will always be top of the heap for me.' 'Oh,' I says, 'then what about that débutante bit, Carol, the one you're always telling me about? That Colonel's daughter.' 'Oh, 'er,' he says, 'she's just a bit of Knightsbridge candy floss. A couple of licks and you've 'ad 'er.' 205 210

There is a long pause. CLEA *is now sitting on the table, swinging her vodka bottle in absolute command.*

COLONEL [*at last grappling with the situation; faintly*] Did you say four years, madam?

CLEA [*in her own voice, quietly*] Yes, Colonel. Four years, in this room.

HAROLD I know that voice. It's Clea! 215

CAROL [*horrified*] Clea!

BRINDSLEY [*unconvincingly*] Clea?

COLONEL I don't understand anything that's going on in this room!

Understanding the text

1 Because farce is concerned with examining 'typical' human failings, the characters tend to represent general types of people rather than believable individuals. One of the ways of quickly indicating this to an audience is in the playwright's choice of character names. What do the names of the characters in this extract suggest about them?

2 The term 'genre' can be used to suggest what 'family of dramas' a particular play belongs to. Think about what sort of music, scenery, costume, make-up and action would tell you in just a few seconds that you were watching a horror movie. Pick out at least three incidents or lines in this extract that show that *Black Comedy* is a farce rather than a slice of real life.

3 In a farce, it is important that the audience do not feel too much sympathy for any of the characters. They are, after all, being set up for the audience to laugh at: feeling too sorry for any of them would perhaps stop us thinking about the daft things that we do and say and how ridiculously we sometimes behave! Consider the different characters in this scene and pick out some examples of things they do or say that would stop an audience feeling too sorry for them.

4 Making a farce really funny for an audience requires split-second timing on the part of the actors. Pick out three moments in this extract where you can see that precision timing is essential to achieve a comic effect.

5   One of the key ingredients of farce is to set up the characters so that they have particular desires and then twist the situation to make sure that they don't get what they want. Make a table for three of the characters in this extract. In one column jot down what they appear to want to happen or achieve. In the next column, make a note of how their wishes are thwarted by the situation.

6   Although this is (when played well) a very funny scene, the play as a whole does set out to make some critical comments about the way people behave. Think of other examples of plays, films or television shows that seem to you to try to make some mildly serious points by poking fun at different types of people.

Producing the scene

1   Draw a plan view of what you think would be an ideal set for this play. Although the action mainly takes place in one room, you will need to read the stage directions very carefully in order to identify what exits and entrances are necessary to achieve the comic comings and goings. Use your own imagination to suggest how the room is decorated and what different pieces of furniture and ornaments Brindsley might have borrowed to make it look as if he is a successful young artist.

2   If the characters' names suggest that they are stereotypes (that is, typical specimens), how might they be costumed in order to help an audience recognise what sort of person they represent? Choose any one of the characters in this extract and design a costume for them. As well as drawing or describing the costume, make notes on why you have chosen to dress them in this way.

3   A good deal of the comedy in Black Comedy obviously comes from the fact that the actors are acting as if they are in complete darkness yet the audience can see everything they are doing. In groups, select a short sequence from the extract where you feel that this theatrical trick could be used to create a lot of laughs. Rehearse the section and discuss in as much detail as you can exactly what the actors have to do to communicate the idea that they are in total darkness.

4   One of the characteristic features of English farce is the use of tableaux. At certain moments the action pauses and the characters stand still just long enough for the audience to inspect their reactions to something by looking at their position on stage and their facial expressions. One example of where a director might choose to set the actors into a tableau would be on the final line, 'I don't understand anything that's going on in this room!' Working in a small group, find two or three other instances when you feel it would be a good idea to momentarily pause the action. Decide what effect you would want to have on an audience at these moments and experiment with ways of positioning the characters and holding their expressions in order to achieve that.

Further development

1   Each member of the group must invent a name which strongly suggests a particular type of character and writes it on a piece of paper. (Harry Enfield's characters Tim Nice-But-Dim and Waynetta Slob are good examples, but make sure you use your own imagination rather than just stealing his ideas!) Each piece of paper is folded once and placed in the middle of a circle, then everyone takes one at random. Form into groups of four or five, then open your piece of paper. Quickly decide where these characters might meet and improvise a scene in which the nature of the different characters becomes obvious.

2   A classic scene in farce involves someone being caught in a compromising position, that is, doing something that would be hard to explain. The fun comes, of course, when they try desperately to give an explanation for the situation they are in. In groups of three, A and B should freeze as if they have been caught redhanded doing something. It may be that what they are doing is genuinely innocent – but it looks as if it is not. Alternatively, it may be that they really shouldn't have been doing what they were doing. Improvise the scene that occurs when C enters and says, 'And just what is going on here?'

3   Make up a scene in which someone has the wool pulled over their eyes, either because they are too stupid or too full of themselves to see what is really going on.

4   In drama we use the word 'hubris' to describe those moments when a character is brought down by their own failing. For example, it would be considered 'hubris' when a politician who has made a big thing about punishing wrong-doers harshly is discovered to have been corrupt themselves and is brought to justice (perhaps you can think of some examples!). What sort of faults really bug you? Greed? Big-headedness? Selfishness? Bitchiness? In groups, devise a scene in which a character that has a particular failing gets their comeuppance in such a way that the audience will think, 'Good – that's no less than they deserve.'

THE GOLDEN PATHWAY ANNUAL

by John Harding and John Burrows

CAST (in order of appearance)

MADEMOISELLE

MICHAEL

THE HEAD

3 speaking parts. No doubling.

If you've come across the term 'baby boom' elsewhere you will know that it refers to the period of fifteen years or so after World War 2 in which the population increased dramatically. There are many different reasons for this sudden growth. Perhaps people thought that the world after the war would be a bright, hopeful place to live in. There was a growing prosperity and the Government strongly urged that a new Britain should rise from the ruins of the old. The 1944 Education Act had improved everyone's chances of getting a decent secondary education and soon colleges and polytechnics were offering higher education to many who, before the war, would have had only a very slim chance of studying at that level. New technology was rapidly changing the world. The race to get man into space started and, with more and more homes acquiring television sets, people became more aware and better informed of what was going on in the world. By the end of the 1950s many people must have been able to see the possibility of an exciting and prosperous future. The 1960s brought all manner of new ideas in art, theatre and education, and technology seemed to develop at an even faster pace.

However, by the end of the 1960s the dream seemed to be fading. There was, for example, widespread rioting in 1968 with students protesting against American involvement in Vietnam. Many thought that although technology was progressing, society was not. Civil Rights movements in both the US and Northern Ireland ended in bloodshed as the protesters challenged the authority of the state. Whereas at the beginning of the decade prospects for employment had been excellent, by the end of it more and more workers were being laid off. Machines were more efficient and more economical; some people began to find that despite their education there was no job waiting for them.

116

The Golden Pathway Annual traces the story of one boy, Michael Peters, through these years, from the return of his father after the war with 'a lovely twinkle' in his eye, up to 1968 when the only job he can get involves sacking his own father.

The style of the play

Overall the play could be described as a comedy; it certainly seems to make the audiences laugh a lot – older people because they are reminded both of the traumas of growing up and the events of the period, and younger ones because they can see Michael having the same trouble with his parents as they are with theirs! The writing is quite straightforward. The play is divided into a series of short scenes depicting key moments in Michael's life. The stage directions suggest that it is played on a conventional proscenium arch stage. Only two chairs and a few props are needed, but an important part of the set is the backdrop which should be a huge Start-Rite Shoes advertisement. The advert shows two young children setting off along a golden road and the slogan below reads: 'Children's shoes have far to go, Start-Rite and they'll walk happily ever after.' As well as being a very nostalgic symbol, the picture represents Michael's story in a sad way; he does 'Start-Rite' but things don't turn out as either he or his parents thought they would.

The extract

As a bright boy Michael would have gone to a grammar school. However, like many adolescents, he is much more interested in his French teacher and the exploits of James Bond (or whoever the current media hero is) than in learning French. In this scene he slips into his own fantasy world. Notice how the writers achieve a great deal of comedy through the unlikely mix of the world of James Bond with Michael's real situation.

––––––––––––

Scene five

1963 Michael Peters, seeing himself as James Bond, takes on 'The Head' and gives the French Assistante more than she bargained for.

Enter MADEMOISELLE *and* MICHAEL.

MLLE Bonjour, Michel. Comment ça va?

MICHAEL   Assez bien, merci, Mademoiselle Leblanc. Et vous?

MLLE   Comme ci, comme ça. Vous êtes seul aujourd'hui?

MICHAEL   Oui. Je cris que les autres sont absents.

MLLE   Eh, bien, la conversation française entre nous deux. Qu'est-ce   5
que vous avez fait cette semaine?

MICHAEL   Presque rien, comme d'habitude: les leçons, les devoirs, rien
de plus.

MLLE   Mais pensez. Nous devons parler. Qu'est ce que vous pensez des
lycéens anglais comme vous?   10

MICHAEL   Er, er, je crois que, je ne suis pas certain de – répétez vous,
s'il vous plaît.

MLLE   Oh Peters! Every week we go through this charade of French
conversation. You always tell me you have done nothing, you are
just a schoolboy, so we talk of autumn, pieces of theatre, la vie   15
française. [*Fantasy begins and* MICHAEL *becomes James Bond for the rest
of scene.*] Let us be frank. You are not Michael Peters, and I am not
Françoise Leblanc. We both know why we are here, and time is getting short. You can trust me, James Bond, 007 of Her Majesty's
Secret Service!   20

MICHAEL   Incroyable! What makes you think I am not Michael
Peters?

MLLE   One or two little things I have noticed. First, there is your
physique: superb. Second, under that ridiculous English schoolboy
blazer you wear a handmade sea island cotton shirt with your black   25
silk knitted tie. Then you do not take school dinners.

MICHAEL   Many of the boys bring a packed lunch.

MLLE   Underdone tournedos à la sauce Béarnaise with coeur d'arti-
chaut and a bottle of Tattainger Blanc de Brut '43?

MICHAEL   So I like good food and drink.   30

MLLE   You overtook the 183 bus this morning on your way to school
in a 1930 4½-litre supercharged Bentley.

MICHAEL   I thought the L plates would fool you.

MLLE   You were wearing your Arnold Riley cap, Bond.

MICHAEL   What are you going to do then, keep me in after school?   35

MLLE   Don't think it hasn't crossed my mind, James. I am your French
contact, Ophelia Plenty.

MICHAEL   All in good time. [*Aside.*] Something about the jutting swell
of her pointed hillocks, her square-toed shoes, and the thick weight
of hair at the nape of the neck told me she was no ordinary French   40
Assistante. How did you get into the Service?

MLLE   My father was a great chef, pressed into service by the Nazis
during the occupation, but he passed on information to the

Resistance. When the Gestapo shot him, my mother, my brothers and sisters, I alone escaped, and vowed to fight always for freedom. 45

MICHAEL Good girl. Did your father serve rognon de veau with pommes sautés followed by fraises des bois?

MLLE Of course. Oh James, it has been an agony, waiting till I could reveal myself. I want you, James. I want you to do everything to me. Everything you've ever done to a woman. Now, please. 50

MICHAEL Certainly, choux-fleure. What have you been able to find out?

MLLE Someone in the school is attempting to brainwash the sixth form.

MICHAEL Right. The boys have been implanted with something 55
which makes them completely servile. It's pathetic: instead of living the life of red-blooded young males, they stay in at night doing homework, they do virtually without money and sex, display amazing anxiety over exams, and are prepared to bully younger boys of their own class in an obsequious desire to please masters. But who 60
is behind it all?

MLLE One of the arch fiends of all time. He's subtle, ruthless, mad, and physically revolting. So important is he in the underworld, they call him The Head.

MICHAEL The Head! Of course, his earlobes are too long, and his fat 65
lips always wet. But what is his aim?

MLLE He wants to rule the world through these automatons, and he holds sway over them with a terrible promise: success. Success that is always just another exam away. Careful, James. The skeleton butt of your .25 Beretta is interfering with the mysterious promise of my 70
folded thighs.

MICHAEL We must liquidate him.

MLLE You do it James. I can watch. When this is all over, we could get married. You do love me just a little, don't you, James?

MICHAEL Thanks for telling me what you know, Miss Plentsky. 75

MLLE James!

MICHAEL You bitch! You're a double agent. You're SMERSH.

MLLE Oh, James, I feel so guilty. How did you know?

MICHAEL Rognon de veau is served with pommes soufflés, not sautés. 80

MLLE But they forced me, James. I love you.

MICHAEL You would have used me to get rid of The Head, then killed me and used his secrets to control innocent schoolboys in Georgia for your own vile communistic ends!

MLLE Oh, it's true! It's true! 85

Enter THE HEAD. *He holds a cane.*

THE HEAD   I congratulate you, Mr Bond. A remarkable piece of deduction. Such a pity it should come to nothing.

MLLE   } The Head!
MICHAEL   }

THE HEAD   I have heard everything, my dear boy. How clever of my old school chum M to infiltrate 007 as a schoolboy. But for Ophelia   90 Plentsky, your cover would remain intact, so I think it only fair that she should die first and leave us boys together, don't you? [*He stabs her with the end of the cane. She dies slowly.*]

MICHAEL   You swine!

THE HEAD   Come, Mr Bond, she is our mutual enemy.   95

MICHAEL   But she is a beautiful woman!

THE HEAD   How touching and quaint that you should fall victim to the weakness of flesh we call lust. You should know never to trust a woman, James. Now she's quiet, we can enjoy ourselves. No heroics please. [*He rips open* MICHAEL*'s shirt, draws blood with cane.*] What   100 fine red blood you have, James. You will write me a thousand lines in it before you die.

MICHAEL   You're mad, The Head!

THE HEAD   Tush, I think 'I must not be a secret agent in class' would be appropriate, don't you?   105

MICHAEL   What do you hope to gain with this scheme of yours?

THE HEAD   Do not play the dull and stupid schoolboy, James. You know you are capable of much better work. I already control the most intelligent young men in England. What is to stop me taking over the world?   110

MICHAEL   Damn the Welfare State!

THE HEAD   Quite. I think perhaps I should cane you to death, no? Drop your trousers. Bend over. [*He is paralysed as he draws his arm back.*] Aagh! But what is happening to me?

MICHAEL   You underestimated me, The Head. As I dropped my   115 trousers, I released a tiny spider stolen from the biology lab. It has bitten your jugular.

THE HEAD   Poisonous insects in the school? The P.T.A. wouldn't allow it.

MICHAEL   On its own, the spider is quite harmless. But the catalyst   120 with which I spiked the staffroom tea makes the venom deadly. I'll take that. [*He seizes* THE HEAD*'s cane.*]

THE HEAD   Finish with me, I beg you.

MICHAEL   Not after the way you dealt with Ophelia. Your agony will
be overwhelming. You have just a few minutes, the only part of your   125
body not paralysed is the larynx. Now talk.

Exit MICHAEL *with Ophelia's corpse.*

Scene six

1964 Speech Day.

THE HEAD *unfreezes and addresses the audience.*

THE HEAD   Well, the Hutchinson Prize for Expertise in Biology
Practical – well done again, Owen – brings us to the end of the main
part of Prize Giving and leaves only our most coveted award. The
Arnold Riley Prize itself, which goes to Michael Peters of the Upper   130
Sixth Arts. And I hope I shan't embarrass Michael too much by saying that the committee meeting to decide who should receive this
award was one of the shortest I have ever had the pleasure of chair-
ing. I know I can rest assured that when, sadly, Michael leaves us at
the end of term, becomes an Old Boy of the school, an Old Arnold   135
Rileyonian, and goes on to higher things at the University, he will
go forth armed with this book as our ambassador, representing all
our hopes and ideals, symbolized completely in the name of Arnold
Riley. Come along, Michael.

He beckons an imaginary MICHAEL *from the audience, then turns to
meet* MICHAEL *for Scene seven.*

Understanding the text

1   At what point in the scene does the daydream actually start? How is this
reflected in what is actually being said?
2   Pick out three lines which should make the audience laugh because they are
absurd or impossible to believe.
3   There are moments in the scene when the audience are reminded that this
is not a 'real' James Bond scene but just Michael playing with the idea. Pick out
two such moments.
4   What do we learn about the characters of Michael and The Head in Scene
Five? Is this changed or developed in any way in Scene Six? If so, how?

Producing the scene

1   What similarities does Mademoiselle have with the standard James Bond heroine? If you were the director of this play, what suggestions could you give to the actress playing the part on how to change from French assistante to Ophelia Plenty? Consider in particular tone of voice, movement and gesture.

2   Why does Michael's daydream start in the first place? Working in groups of three with one person playing Michael, one playing Mademoiselle and one as a director, experiment with ways of showing the change. Compare the effect of making the change suddenly at the point where the stage direction reads *Fantasy begins* or working into it gradually from the start of Mademoiselle's speech.

3   How could the actors be positioned in order to achieve a comic effect on the line: 'Careful, James. The skeleton butt of your .25 Beretta is interfering with the mysterious promise of my folded thighs'? In pairs, imagine you are posing for a publicity photograph designed to show that the play is a comedy.

4   Design or describe a suitable costume for The Head. Would you consider what your own headteacher wears as a good choice or is your immediate thought to produce something different? Give reasons for your final choice.

5   The stage direction: *He rips open Michael's shirt, draws blood with cane* could be achieved in a number of ways. Suggest two possible methods of dealing with this and weigh up the advantages and disadvantages of each.

6   What effect does the stage direction: *The Head unfreezes and addresses the audience* have on that audience? What other devices could you use at this point to help the audience understand that we have shifted in time and place?

Further development

1   What other common subjects of daydreams might be suitable for theatrical treatment along these lines? Prepare a short improvisation in which a character drifts off into a daydream with embarrassing or comic results.

2   Find a space in the room on your own and think of a character from any film or TV adventure series. After one minute's thinking time the teacher or group leader should clap her hands, at which point you must:
  •   start improvising as that character
  •   move around the room in search of someone else from the same film or series (it may be another version of your choice)
  •   when you find her, continue improvising together.

3   A number of stories deal with characters who have some trouble separating fact from fiction. You may know books like *Billy Liar* or *The Secret Life of Walter Mitty*. Invent a character who is an incurable liar or daydreamer. In pairs improvise a scene in which the character has been sent to a psychiatrist and is asked

to tell how this trait has got her into trouble. The person playing the psychiatrist can help the scene to develop by asking questions which demand detailed answers.

4   In groups of four to six develop some of the ideas generated in Question 3 into 'flashback' scenes.

5   One of the reasons for the success of *The Golden Pathway Annual* is its use of nostalgia. People seem to love wallowing in memories of their youth! As a whole class, imagine yourselves attending a class reunion in fifty years' time. Remember that memories often become more fantastic than the original event. Remind each other, in your improvisation, of some of the amazing characters and incidents of your school days.

6   Following on from Question 5, researching into what your parents or grandparents remember from their youth could provide you with material for a longer piece of work. It would be interesting, for example, to see if their lives fit into the pattern of life described at the start of this chapter. Are they 'baby boomers'? How do they remember the 1960s? Prepare an improvisation which reflects life in the 1980s as you see it.

7   Characters like The Head are often referred to as 'stock characters' or stereotypes. Consider the way comics, cartoons and many popular comedies depict policemen, mothers-in-law and drunkards. What other characters are often stereotyped? Choose a number of stereotypes and invent a scene in which one or several of them confront 'normal', non-stereotyped people in the real world.

THE BODY

by Nick Darke

CAST (in order of appearance)

3 FARMERS

KENNETH

GRACE

ALICE

MRS MAY

ARCHIE GROSS

GILBERT

RECTOR

10 speaking parts. Doubling possible.

Identifying exactly what it is about something that makes us laugh is very difficult. Sometimes we laugh because we feel a kind of sympathy for the characters; if they are in an unfortunate situation we feel a kind of relief that it is them and not us, although we might remember that we have been in similar situations ourselves. Sometimes we laugh because we enjoy seeing someone get her comeuppance; there is a bit of difference between seeing a stingy millionaire slip on a banana skin and seeing a frail old lady do so.

The Body is, I think, a completely different kind of comedy. For some strange reason we laugh at the inability of human beings to get things right. Perhaps we feel sympathy for ourselves for being members of such a woefully confused species! The play could be described as a 'black comedy' in that underlying the crazy story-line it is making some very bitter comments, and at the end of the play the comedy seems to dissolve altogether, making us wonder what it was that we were laughing about. It is the story of a village in Cornwall which has an American weapons base as a neighbour. The villagers' lives and interests seem trivial, yet they appear, on the whole, content with their lot. The Americans, on the other hand, are crying out for something interesting to happen in order to justify their presence in such a dull place. When one of the American soldiers literally drops dead with boredom it sets off a chain of events which include conscription of one of the locals to fill his place, the arrest of most of the villagers as communist infiltrators, and a major, possibly apocalyptic, international crisis.

The style of the play

The play moves rapidly from one scene to another and was designed for a simple, easily rearranged set. A group of farmers act as a chorus throughout the play and, just like the traditional chorus in a Greek play, they fill in details, comment on the action and speculate on what will happen next. The characterisation of both the locals and Americans is rather unsubtle – they seem to be stereotypes rather than 'real' people, which makes the play both funnier and more pointed in its message.

The extract

This is the opening section of the play. As you will see, a number of characters are introduced in quick succession and the action jumps from one place to another. The play launches straight into the action and clearly the audience will have to be alert in order to take it all in.

———————————

Prologue

   Three FARMERS *of the parish address the audience.*

FARMERS   We, the farmers of this parish,
   Do admit
   The presence of
   American units
   On our airbase.   5
   We look out across
   Our meadows
   And count
   Nuclear weapons
   Amongst our sheep.   10
   We speak with one voice
   And keep our collective
   Mouth on the subject shut.
   We have no choice,
   We know that.   15

And we gaze with mild disapproval
Upon those who seek their removal.

One of our number, Kenneth, sat with his wife one morning, before breakfast.

KENNETH *removes himself from the* FARMERS' *group and sits with his wife,* GRACE. *She joints a bullock.*

KENNETH   Grace, I fancy mushrooms for breakfast.   20
GRACE   Then pick some.
KENNETH   I think I might. That's what I was thinking.
GRACE   Did you milk the cows?
KENNETH   Yes.
GRACE   Feed the pigs?   25
KENNETH   Yes.
GRACE   Count the sheep?
KENNETH   Yes.
GRACE   Collect the eggs?
KENNETH   Yes.   30
GRACE   Grease the combine?
KENNETH   I can't grease the combine Grace, not before breakfast, on an empty stomach.
GRACE   Then don't leave it for me to do at the last minute. I can't reach the nipples. There's nipples on that combine was put in places   35 a cockroach couldn' reach.
KENNETH   My arms is too thick. Yours is thinner.
GRACE   My bosom get in the way.
KENNETH   Then diet.
GRACE   I aren't goin' on a diet so you dun' ave to grease the combine.   40
KENNETH   Good a reason as any.
GRACE   And dun't forget the dance tomorrer night.
KENNETH   Tch!
GRACE   Lookin' forward to that.
KENNETH   The best field for pickin' mushrooms on my farm backs on   45 to the airforce base.
GRACE   Be careful.
KENNETH   I tell you what I'll do. I'll keep my bedroom slippers on. It's a light dew and they won't get wet, and the Yanks will take me for what I am. A plain English farmer.   50
GRACE   Don't bank on it.
KENNETH   I'll be as long as it takes me to pick a grain pan full of mushrooms.

KENNETH *goes.* GRACE *sits. Music plays, then stops.* GRACE *looks at her watch.*

GRACE He's late.

Music plays again. GRACE *uncrosses her legs and re-crosses them the other way. Music stops. She looks at her watch.*

GRACE He's bin gone a day now. Twenty-four hours. I think I'm get- 55
tin' worried. Soon be time to make enquiries. Start askin' round a bit.

She goes. Music intro to FARMERS' *song.*

Part one

The FARMERS *of the parish sing a song.*

FARMERS The farmers of this parish
Would dearly love to tell,
All about Mother May 60
A body and a – well,
Mother May went cocklin',
No, we haven't started right,
To get the yarn out viddy
We got to start the night 65
Before,
When Stanly stuck her bloomers
In the roof to stop the leak,
So she could take the bucket out
From underneath. 70
So now she got the *bucket*
To do with what she like,
And with the *bucket* in er 'and
She set sail on her bike.
Bike got a puncture 75
So she ayved'n in the ditch,
Decide to pick some cockles
From beneath the iron bridge.
Now *this* is where the story start,
With the cockles, and the *body*, 80
And Alice, and the iron bridge,
The bucket, and the . . .

MRS MAY *and* ALICE *walking marchez sur place.* MRS MAY *muddy to the knee and carrying a bucket full of cockles.*

ALICE   Mornin' Mrs May.

MAY   Mornin' Alice.

ALICE   Hear the larks?   85

MAY   Lovely.

ALICE   You'm lookin' rosy Mrs May.

MAY   Thank you.

ALICE   Like you bin stridin' against the wind.

MAY   Bin over the cliff.   90

ALICE   You'm muddy half way to the knee.

MAY   Ah. Bin in the mud.

ALICE   And you have in your hand a bucket.

MAY   There now.

ALICE   Bin cocklin'?   95

MAY   Observant Alice.

ALICE   Bin under th'iron bridge?

MAY   Iron bridge Alice yes.

ALICE   Iron bridge is it?

MAY   And I've found more'n cockles.   100

ALICE   People often do, under th'iron bridge.

MAY   I was jabbin' about with me toes in the mud, jabbin' about for a cockle,

ALICE   Ez . . .

MAY   And me foot oozed on summin soft.   105

ALICE   Flesh.

MAY   I gived it a prod with me stick and it felt like Stanly's belly.

ALICE   Twad'n Stanly . . .

MAY   An' I put me 'and down, and twined me finger in a strand of seaweed.   110

ALICE   Hair . . .

MAY   'Twas a body, what I found beneath th'iron bridge.

ALICE   Dead?

MAY   As a doormat.

     ALICE *stops to consider this and* MRS MAY *stops also.*

ALICE   Still there is 'e?   115

MAY   I ab'm brung the bugger 'ome in the bucket.

ALICE   Just the one was it?

MAY   How many do 'e want?

ALICE   Better inform an authority ad'n'e?

MAY   I will do Alice, after I've 'ad me photograph took with it.   120

ALICE   'Ere come Archie Gross. Inform 'e.

MAY   I dun't inform Archie Gross a nothin'. Me an' 'e dun't mix.

ALICE   Inform Gilbert. Policeman.

MAY   I will do Alice. But that there body belong to me. So dun't you
go yakkin'.   125

> ARCHIE GROSS *walking marchez sur place. He carries an empty*
> *bucket.*

GROSS   Archie Gross, you're a lucky man. The sun's shinin' and the
larks are singin'. You've an empty bucket in your 'and, danglin', by
the side, swingin' fore an' back in time with a loose and easy gait,
which is step by step drawin' 'e closer to the cockle beds below the
iron bridge. And there id'n nothin' like a bucket fulla cockles in the   130
world, bar a good eggy tart like Tysie make. Aw. Cloud loomin' on
the horizon, in the bulbous shape a Mrs May. She bring rain to me,
she an' me dun't conglomerate. Look like she bin cocklin', so thass
summin I d'know 'bout 'er. Less she knaw 'bout me less she can yack
around the parish. And there's Alice with 'er, sprig a blossom   135
brought out be the rain.

> *They converge.*

Mornin' Mrs May.

MAY   So they say.

GROSS [*raising his hat*]   Mornin' Alice.

ALICE   Mornin', Mr Gross.   140

GROSS   Hear the larks?

ALICE   Lovely.

GROSS   Bin for a jaunt?

MAY   There and back. Whass that bucket?

GROSS   Ohh, 'tis a bucket.   145

MAY   I noticed, you carry a bucket.

GROSS   I could say the same about you.

MAY   But I'm on me way back. You'm on your way.

GROSS   Ah, I'm er, goin' to milk the cow.

MAY   Out here?   150

GROSS   I have a cow, by name a Buttercup, who wander.

MAY   I hope she yield a good gallon.

> *They pass.*

FARMERS [*sing*]   So off they went
   To East and West
   With little said   155
   And love lost less
   Mr Gross had told a fib,

Proper little whopper
Mrs May and Alice went
To winkle out a copper.   160

> GILBERT *stands at the station desk. A pile of dollar bills and a box of*
> *popcorn sit on the desk-top.* GILBERT *eats popcorn. He closes the book*
> *and buttons up his jacket.* MRS MAY *strides in followed by* ALICE.

GILBERT   Mornin' Mrs May.
MAY   Now thun.
GILBERT   Mornin' Alice.
ALICE   Mmmmmmmmmmmmmmmmm.
MAY   Gilbert.   165
ALICE   Mmmmmmmmmmm.
MAY   Gilbert.
GILBERT   Goin' dance tonight?
MAY   Got summin for 'e. Now listen 'ere boy . . .
ALICE   What dance?   170
GILBERT   Parish 'all.
ALICE   Dance tonight, is there?
MAY   Gilbert . . .
GILBERT   Goin'?
MAY   Gilbert.   175
ALICE   Mmmmmmm. Who's playin'?
GILBERT   Manny Cockle and the Big Four Combo.
ALICE   Ooh.
MAY   Gilbert.
ALICE   You gonna take me?   180
GILBERT   Mmmmmmmmmm.
MAY   Christ!
ALICE   Cus I got to go now . . .
MAY   Alice will you stop yakkin' maid!
GILBERT   Where to?   185
ALICE   Eat me dinner.
MAY   Gilbert you on duty or no?
GILBERT   What 'e got for dinner?
MAY   GILBERT!
ALICE   Eggy tart.   190

> ALICE *goes.*

MAY   *Now* thun!
GILBERT   Eh?
MAY   I found a dead body cocklin'.

130

GILBERT   Whass a dead body doin' cocklin'.
MAY   I was cocklin', the body was dead.   195
GILBERT   Where to?
MAY   Iron bridge.
GILBERT   Under'n?
MAY   Ez you, under'n.
GILBERT   Hell. Whose body is it?   200
MAY   I dunnaw. E'm washed up more like. Up the estuary, out the sea.
GILBERT   Aw.
MAY   You comin' or no!
GILBERT   I got 'ave me dinner.
MAY   Gaw damme boy 'twill be washed out again time you've 'ad your   205
   dinner!
GILBERT [*not enthusiastic*]   Come on thun.

   They go.

FARMERS [*sing*]   Gilbert was reluctant,
   To say the very least,
   To go and dig up bodies   210
   Where bodies don't exist.
   But before we carry on with them,
   We've raced a bit ahead,
   We must return to Mr Gross,
   Who *at* the cockle beds.   215

   ARCHIE GROSS *cockling. He sits, removes his boots and rolls his
   trousers up. Checks the independence of his toes, walks a bit and whistles quietly to himself. Suddenly he plunges his foot into the mud, and
   feels for a cockle. Then his plunges his other foot, and he is cockling.
   He sings . . .*

GROSS   There is nothing like a cockle . . . We are poor black cockles,
   who have lost our way . . . Old man cockle . . . Cockles in the night
   . . . Red cockles in the sunset . . . Once, I had a secret cockle . . .
   123 o'clock 4 o'clock cockle, 567 o'clock 8 o'clock cockle I'm gonna
   rock, around, the cockle tonight . . .   220

   *His foot action turns into the twist and he is carried away. Then he
   stops, his face changes, and he feels very carefully with his toes. He's
   found the* BODY.

GROSS   Hell.

He starts to edge his feet horizontally along the BODY, *stopping at significant places. At last he gets to the head.*

Body.

He feels some more.

Dead. Damme. Now what. Shift'n. Handcart. Take'n church. Inform the rector.

GROSS goes off. He leaves the BODY *lying there. The* BODY *is covered from head to toe with mud.*

FARMERS [*sing*]   Now this is where our story start   225
To gather its momentum,
Mr Gross and handcart
Were there and back in no time.

GROSS comes back with a handcart. He lifts the BODY *on and off as they sing.*

The body lifted off the flats
And placed with haste   230
Upon the trap.
Mrs May, with rumblin' gait,
Arrived with Gilbert,
A mite too late.

MRS MAY and GILBERT arrive on the scene, panting. She looks around her, conducts the proceedings like a military exercise.

MAY   Take your boots and stockin's off boy.   235
GILBERT   Eh?

She hitches her skirts and plunges her foot in the mud.

MAY   Plunge your foot in.
GILBERT   Eh?
MAY   Got 'ome 'twas rainin'. Said to Stanly, 'Where's me bloomer?' 'E
said, 'Stoppin' up the leak in the roof.' I said, 'Proper job, cockles for   240
tea.' Plunge your foot in boy.

She plunges her other foot.

This is the spot. He'm down 'ere.

She feels about. No BODY.

Damme e'm sunk.

GILBERT   Eh?

MAY   Take your trousers off boy.   245

GILBERT   [*taking off his trousers*]   Eh?

MAY   'E've gone deep. 'Ave a probe a bit.

GILBERT   Who's the policeman around 'ere.

MAY   *There* now.

GILBERT   What now?   250

MAY   That there body . . .'s vanished.

GILBERT   Gyat. Twad'n never there. 'Tis a figment.

MAY   Praise the lord! E'm a Lazarus! E've took up his bed an' walked!
   Advance with me Gilbert! To the rector!

> *And she's gone.* GILBERT *picks up his trousers and follows.* ARCHIE
> GROSS, *pulling his hand cart.*

FARMERS   [*sing*]   With flying skirt   255
   And rolling lurch
   She forged a path
   Toward the church
   With Gilbert, close behind.
   Over hill   260
   And down the dip,
   Archie Gross
   Cracked his whip
   And galloped with his find.

GROSS   Archie Gross, you'm a lucky man. You set out this mornin'   265
   with nothin' more in mind 'n' a handsome bucket fulla cockles, and
   here y'are returnin' 'ome with a cartload a dead body! Hero a the
   parish! I'll have 'em all yakkin'. An' Mrs May steamin' like a silage
   pit for lettin' a dead body through her toes while jabbin' for a cockle
   beneath the iron bridge. She think she'm the big I am, but who   270
   found the body!

> *The* BODY *slips off the back of the cart.*

FARMERS   [*sing*]   No sooner had he said those words,
   He reached an incline in the road,
   Steeper steeper climbed the cart,
   And the body slipped off onto the path.   275

> *The church. The* RECTOR *stands by the lych gate dressed as a*
> *Chinaman.* ARCHIE GROSS *arrives with his empty cart.*

GROSS   Rector! I see you're dressed as a Chinaman.

RECTOR   Observant Archie.

GROSS   And the church seem somewhat altered.

RECTOR   On the outside.

GROSS   Now thun.   280

RECTOR   The nave is exactly as you might remember it.

GROSS   Got summin show 'e.

RECTOR   You see Archie it started with the fund raisin'.

GROSS   Twad'n me who stripped the lead off the steeple.

RECTOR   No 'twas the October gale.   285

GROSS   I lost a dutch barn in that one . . . now look 'ere look, in the 'and cart . . .

RECTOR   I said to Jack Steeple the steeplejack that steeple, Jack, is leakin'. Jack Steeple looked at me and then 'e eyed the steeple. Rector, said Jack, the leak in that steeple is gonna take some stop-   290 pin'. The steeple's bent. I could erect a pagoda cheaper. A pagoda said I. Aye said Jack. A pagoda. I looked at Jack, then I eyed the steeple. All the while my 'and clasped the forty seb'm an'sixpence, the parish response to my appeal, includin' bingo, and I said to meself, so Jack couldn' 'ear, nuts. For all the attention I get on a   295 Sunday mornin' I might as well be a Chinaman, so here I am, pagoda, Chinese cassock wi' dragons on, and pointed hat. And do you know Archie? You're the first bugger who's noticed.

GROSS   Then rector 'tis your lucky day. There's a body in the back a that cart!   300

RECTOR   Lead me to it!

GROSS   Follow.

> ARCHIE GROSS *leads the* RECTOR *round to the back of the cart. The cart is empty.*

Aw. Aw my gor.

RECTOR   Dearodear.

GROSS   I tell 'e Rector 'e was 'ere! Dead as a doormat, lyin' in the back   305 a the cart!

RECTOR   Come inside the pagoda Archie, an' I'll relieve 'e of a sin or two, you'm clearly in need of spiritual aid.

GROSS   'Tis Mrs May. She'm a witch.

RECTOR   Mrs May is a stalwart of the parish.   310

GROSS   She'll stop a pig bleedin' a mile off, I seed 'er do it!

RECTOR   She has a shiny pew, through constant use Archie, I'm sur- prised you found your way here.

GROSS   She spirited the bugger off the cart, set the parish yakkin!

Understanding the text

1   Pick out six examples of where the playwright has tried to capture the accent of the local characters. Give a reason why this might be important in this first scene. What immediate effect does it have on the reader or audience?

2   How would you describe the relationship between Mrs May and Archie Gross as it is outlined in this opening scene? What impression do you get of:
- their age
- their position in the community
- their opinion of each other?

3   What sort of character is Gilbert? Is there anything about his appearance on the stage that suggests we shouldn't take him too seriously as a policeman?

4   Explain, in your own words, why the Rector is dressed as a Chinaman. Look at Archie's first comment to him. What does this suggest to you about the characters in this village and Archie in particular?

5   What do you understand by the word 'stereotype'? Make a list of the qualities you would expect to see in:
- a stereotyped farmer or 'yokel'
- a stereotyped policeman
- a stereotyped village gossip.

Find lines in the script, or make up some lines, that you think fit such a characterisation well.

Producing the scene

1   Draw a picture of or describe the three farmers in order to show how you would use costume and make-up to create a stereotype. What advice could you give the actors about movement, mannerisms and tone of voice to help bring your drawing to life?

2   Design a costume for the Rector. What problems might you face if you had to actually make such a costume?

3   List at least four properties (props) that you would need to find in order to produce this scene, and design them. Say who they would be used by and whether you think they are the sort of things that could be found or would have to be specially made.

4   List the different places around the village that need to be shown in these opening scenes. How could you suggest each one simply and arrange the stage so that you could move from one piece of action to the next without slowing down the pace of the scene?

5   No lights are specified for this scene, but using lights might help the audience to understand when the action is shifting in terms of time and place. Look at

your answer to Question 4 and suggest what sort of lights could be used – and where – in order to make the scene clearer.

6   Look carefully at the scene where Archie discovers the body. How could you achieve this on stage? (Think particularly about whether the body needs to be concealed and, if so, how this could be done.) Act out the scene, experimenting with the timing. How long should Archie do the twist before he finds the body? How quickly should he realise what he has found?

7   Much of the comedy in this scene seems to come from incongruity. The characters often react to things in an unexpected and inappropriate way. Pick out three lines or incidents which you think show this and suggest how the actors on stage could act in order to accentuate the comedy. Try out your suggestions in action to test if they work.

8   What sort of music would you choose for the links in this scene if it wasn't possible to have a live band?

Further development

1   Although it is suggested that the Farmers sing their lines, another technique might be to use choral speech. Pick at least one of their speeches and experiment with ways of producing it as a chorus. Experiment with ways of breaking the speech up so that some lines are spoken by all three Farmers but others are spoken individually. Try exaggerating the accents, rhythm, rhyme and tones of voice to make it funnier.

2   In groups of three or four invent a scene in which the characters are doing something very ordinary, say, fishing, working in a factory or sitting in a launderette. Developing the idea of choral speech, write and present a commentary on the action. Perhaps, at some point, something extraordinary happens. Rather than being shocked, the characters react calmly and comment on it through the use of choral speech.

3   The scene in the police station could be made to be very funny. It works by both Mrs May and Alice trying to talk to Gilbert about two completely different things. Divide into groups of three and improvise a scene in which A is trying to tell B something extremely important. However, B is more interested in carrying on a trivial conversation with C. This could be further developed into a scene in which all three characters are saying something different and not paying attention to whether or not they are being listened to. Devise a way of ending such an improvisation in which the characters realise that what they have said hasn't been heard.

4   *The Body* is a play which tries to make some very serious points through using comedy. Can you think of any television programmes or films which do the same? In groups decide on an issue which you feel strongly about. Devise a scene in which you make serious points about the issue by using comedy.

5   Some of the comedy in the play seems to come purely from the way the characters talk. How aware are you of your own accent? Have you ever heard anyone try to mimic it, and if so, what sort of things have they emphasised? Imagine that the BBC have decided to set a series in your area which depicts everyday life in a comic way by over-emphasising the local accent. Either act out the scene as you think they might do it, or improvise a scene in which you are protesting to the director about the way local characters are portrayed. With the help of the class teacher it could be interesting to devise a confrontation between the actors in the series and the locals which illustrates some of the attitudes to regional accents and ways of life.

THE TAMING OF THE SHREW

by William Shakespeare

CAST (in order of appearance)

BIONDELLO

LUCENTIO

BIANCA

GREMIO

PETRUCHIO

KATE

VINCENTIO

*GRUMIO

PEDANT

BAPTISTA

TRANIO

*OFFICER

*ATTENDANTS AND SERVANTS

10 speaking parts. Doubling possible.
*Non-speaking parts.

This play remains one of Shakespeare's most popular comedies although it is also one of the most criticised. Its central story concerns how a young man – Petruchio – marries a headstrong young woman – Katherina (Kate) – as a bet. All the men in the town are terrified of Kate, who shows herself to be highly independent in a period when women were expected to be totally subservient. Petruchio, however, is arrogant enough to believe that he can 'tame' her. On their first meeting she tries various tricks to frighten him away, but he treats her insults as tokens of love and insists on an early marriage. Her father, Baptista, is delighted to have her off his hands and the incredulous Kate finds herself taken off by Petruchio to his country house. Her 'taming' is achieved by a series of psychological assaults and tricks. At the end of the play she demonstrates her love for her husband in a speech which appears to suggest that she is now pre-pared to be an obedient wife. Everyone is amazed.

In recent years *The Taming of the Shrew* has been branded a chauvinistic play, the harsh humour of which reflects an age in which women had less freedom than they do now. But we should not forget that situation comedies today cast women in the stereotyped role of the tyrant (think of all those mother-in-law jokes on TV!). We live, after all, in a society in which wife beating still exists. Was a woman's lot really tougher in Shakespeare's time? Maybe men still like to see themselves as 'taming' women in the way Petruchio does.

Perhaps the most controversial part of the play for a twenty-first-century audience is Kate's statement of wifely obedience in the final scene of the play, where she seems to be saying that a woman's role in a marriage should be totally subservient. Faced with this, some people prefer to seek an alternative interpretation. They might contrast the superficial romance between Kate's sister (Bianca) and Lucentio, and the true love that develops between Kate and Petruchio. The individual reader or theatregoer can interpret what Shakespeare wrote however she likes. The headache for the director who decides to put on *The Taming of the Shrew* is how to present the play without offending modern – and in particular female – audiences.

The style of the play

In many ways the strengths of the play lie not so much in the creation of believable characters as in the complex plot which sets up all sorts of traps and situations from which the characters have either to escape themselves or be rescued. In this sense it is a forerunner of farce and the modern 'situation comedy' that can be seen on television almost every night.

The extract

Lucentio is a young man who has gone to Padua to study but has fallen in love with Bianca. In order to woo her he disguises himself as her schoolmaster and calls himself Cambio. He instructs his servant, Tranio, to take his own place in the town. So Cambio is really Lucentio and the person who says he is Lucentio is really his servant, Tranio. Gremio is a rival suitor to Bianca; Biondello is another of Lucentio's servants who has pledged to keep his master's secret. Baptista is Bianca's father, and Grumio is Petruchio's servant. In order to give himself more credibility in the town, Lucentio has persuaded a travelling Pedant to pretend he is his father, Vincentio. In this scene the real Vincentio arrives in the town to see his son, having met Petruchio and Kate on the road. This is the penultimate scene of the play in which all the various deceptions and disguises are finally exposed.

Act V Scene 1

Padua. The street in front of LUCENTIO's *house.*

Enter BIONDELLO, LUCENTIO (*as* CAMBIO), *and* BIANCA; GREMIO *is out before.*

BIONDELLO   Softly and swiftly, sir, for the priest is ready.

LUCENTIO   I fly, Biondello. But they may chance to need thee at home; therefore leave us.

Exit (with BIANCA).

BIONDELLO   Nay, faith, I'll see the church a your back, and then come back to my master's as soon as I can. [*Exit.*]   5

GREMIO   I marvel Cambio comes not all this while.

Enter PETRUCHIO, KATE, VINCENTIO, *and* GRUMIO, *with* ATTEN-
DANTS.

PETRUCHIO   Sir, here's the door, this is Lucentio's house.
My father's bears more towards the marketplace;
Thither must I, and here I leave you, sir.

VINCENTIO   You shall not choose but drink before you go.   10
I think I shall command your welcome here,
And by all likelihood some cheer is toward. [*Knock.*]

GREMIO   They're busy within. You were best knock louder.

PEDANT (*as* VINCENTIO) *looks out of the window (above).*

PEDANT   What's he that knocks as he would beat down the gate?

VINCENTIO   Is Signior Lucentio within, sir?   15

PEDANT   He's within, sir, but not to be spoken withal.*

VINCENTIO   What if a man bring him a hundred pound or two, to make merry withal?

PEDANT   Keep your hundred pounds to yourself; he shall need none so long as I live.   20

PETRUCHIO   Nay, I told you your son was well beloved in Padua. Do you hear, sir? To leave frivolous circumstances, I pray you tell Signior Lucentio that his father is come from Pisa and is here at the door to speak with him.

PEDANT   Thou liest. His father is come from Padua and here looking   25
out at the window.

VINCENTIO   Art thou his father?

withal   with

PEDANT   Ay sir, so his mother says, if I may believe her.

PETRUCHIO [*to* VINCENTIO]   Why how now, gentleman? Why this is
flat* knavery, to take upon you another man's name.   30

PEDANT   Lay hands on the villain. I believe 'a* means to cozen*
somebody in this city under my countenance.

    Enter BIONDELLO.

BIONDELLO   I have seen them in the church together; God send 'em
good shipping! But who is here? Mine old master, Vincentio! Now
we are undone and brought to nothing.   35

VINCENTIO   Come hither, crack-hemp.*

BIONDELLO   I hope I may choose, sir.

VINCENTIO   Come hither, you rogue. What, have you forgot me?

BIONDELLO   Forgot you? No, sir. I could not forget you, for I never saw
you before in all my life.   40

VINCENTIO   What, you notorious villain, didst thou never see thy
master's father, Vincentio?

BIONDELLO   What, my old worshipful old master? Yes, marry, sir, see
where he looks out of the window.

VINCENTIO   Is't so, indeed? [*He beats* BIONDELLO.]   45

BIONDELLO   Help, help, help! Here's a madman will murder me.
[*Exit.*]

PEDANT   Help, son! Help, Signior Baptista! [*Exit from above.*]

PETRUCHIO   Prithee, Kate, let's stand aside and see the end of this
controversy. [*They stand aside.*]   50

    Enter PEDANT (*below*) *with* SERVANTS, BAPTISTA, *and* TRANIO (*as*
    LUCENTIO).

TRANIO   Sir, what are you that offer to beat my servant?

VINCENTIO   What am I, sir? Nay, what are you, sir? O immortal gods!
O fine villain! A silken doublet, a velvet horse, a scarlet cloak, and
a copatain* hat! O, I am undone, I am undone! While I play the
good husband at home, my son and my servant spend all at the uni-   55
versity.

TRANIO   How now, what's the matter?

BAPTISTA   What, is the man lunatic?

flat   complete
'a   he
cozen   trick
crack-hemp   villain
copatain   tall and conical

TRANIO   Sir, you seem a sober ancient gentleman by your habit,* but your words show you a madman. Why sir, what 'cerns it you if I wear   60
pearl and gold? I thank my good father, I am able to maintain it.

VINCENTIO   Thy father! O villain, he is a sailmaker in Bergamo.

BAPTISTA   You mistake, sir, you mistake, sir. Pray, what do you think is his name?

VINCENTIO   His name! As if I knew not his name! I have brought him   65
up ever since he was three years old, and his name is Tranio.

PEDANT   Away, away, mad ass! His name is Lucentio, and he is mine only son and heir to the lands of me, Signior Vincentio.

VINCENTIO   Lucentio! O he hath murd'red his master. Lay hold on him, I charge you in the Duke's name. O my son, my son! Tell me,   70
thou villain, where is my son Lucentio?

TRANIO   Call forth an officer. [Enter an OFFICER.] Carry this mad knave to the jail. Father Baptista, I charge you see that he be forth-coming.

VINCENTIO   Carry me to the jail!   75

GREMIO   Stay, officer. He shall not go to prison.

BAPTISTA   Talk not, Signior Gremio. I say he shall go to prison.

GREMIO   Take heed, Signior Baptista, lest you be cony-catched* in this business. I dare swear this is the right Vincentio.

PEDANT   Swear, if thou dar'st.   80

GREMIO   Nay, I dare not swear it.

TRANIO   Then thou wert best say that I am not Lucentio.

GREMIO   Yes, I know thee to be Signior Lucentio.

BAPTISTA   Away with the dotard,* to the jail with him!

VINCENTIO   Thus strangers may be haled* and abused. O monstrous   85
villain!

Enter BIONDELLO, LUCENTIO, *and* BIANCA.

BIONDELLO   Oh we are spoiled – and yonder he is. Deny him, forswear him, or else we are all undone.

Exit BIONDELLO, TRANIO, *and* PEDANT *as fast as may be.*

LUCENTIO   Pardon, sweet father. [*Kneel.*]

VINCENTIO   Lives my sweet son?

BIANCA   Pardon, dear father.

habit   manner
cony-catched   tricked
dotard   old fool
haled   pulled about

142

BAPTISTA How has thou offended? 90
Where is Lucentio?
LUCENTIO Here's Lucentio,
Right son to the right Vincentio,
That have by marriage made thy daughter mine
While counterfeit supposes* bleared thine eyne.*
GREMIO Here's packing, with a witness,* to deceive us all! 95
VINCENTIO Where is that damned villain Tranio
That faced and braved me in this matter so?
BAPTISTA Why, tell me, is not this my Cambio?
BIANCA Cambio is changed into Lucentio.
LUCENTIO Love wrought these miracles. Bianca's love 100
Made me exchange my state with Tranio
While he did bear my countenanance in the town,
And happily I have arrived at the last
Unto the wished haven of my bliss.
What Tranio did, myself enforced him to. 105
Then pardon him, sweet father, for my sake.
VINCENTIO I'll slit the villain's nose that would have sent me to the
jail.
BAPTISTA [to LUCENTIO] But do you hear, sir? Have you married my
daughter without asking my good will? 110
VINCENTIO Fear not, Baptista; we will content you, go to. But I will
in, to be revenged for this villainy. [Exit.]
BAPTISTA And I, to sound the depth of this knavery. [Exit.]
LUCENTIO Look not pale, Bianca. Thy father will not frown. [Exeunt
LUCENTIO and BIANCA.] 115
GREMIO My cake is dough,* but I'll in among the rest
Out of hope of all but my share of the feast. [Exit.]
KATE Husband, let's follow, to see the end of this ado.
PETRUCHIO First kiss me, Kate, and we will.
KATE What, in the midst of the street? 120
PETRUCHIO What, are thou ashamed of me?
KATE No sir, God forbid, but ashamed to kiss.
PETRUCHIO Why, then let's home again. [To GRUMIO.] Come sirrah,
let's away.
KATE Nay, I will give thee a kiss. Now pray thee, love, stay. 125

supposes pretences
eyne eyes
packing, with a witness flagrant deceit
My cake is dough my plans have failed

PETRUCHIO   Is not this well? Come, my sweet Kate. Better once than
   never, for never too late. [*Exeunt.*]

Understanding the text

1   Draw a diagram which shows the names of all the characters in this scene
and how they are connected to each other. This is a bit like drawing a family tree
(only possibly more complicated!).

2   Where are Lucentio and Bianca going at the start of this scene?

3   Pick out the exact moment at which the scene climaxes, that is, the moment
when the problem is at its most acute. How is it resolved in the script? State, in
your own words, what each character intends to do next.

4   Go through the extract and pick out all of the insults which people throw at
each other. (Shakespeare had a vast repertoire of imaginative insults which it is
well worth researching into.) Do these add comedy or are they just spiteful?

5   In what ways do you think this scene is like some situation comedies you
know from television?

Producing the scene

1   What requirements should a set design meet for this scene? Read it through
again carefully and note the actual structure that needs to be present. Sketch a
design which would meet these requirements.

2   Try to work out ways of moving the characters around in this scene. You
could do this either by drawing a plan view of the set you sketched in Question
1 and using letters or coloured dots to represent the characters, or, even better,
by marking out a space on the floor to represent the set and working out the
movements in groups.

3   Where would you place Kate and Petruchio after the stage direction *They
stand aside*? Although they only play a small part in this scene they are important
characters in the play as a whole. What advice would you give them about how
to act or react in this scene?

4   A scene such as this in which people are pretending to be someone else can
be very confusing for an audience. If you had to direct this scene are there any
methods you could use that might help the audience follow it more easily?
Characters could use different voices, movements or facial expressions depending on whether they are addressing a character whom they are trying to take in,
or the audience (who are aware of the deception that is taking place). Choose a

section of no more than twenty lines from the extract (the section from the entrance of Biondello to the entrance of Pedant would be particularly suitable) and make detailed notes as to how you would direct that section.

5   Find out what a 'double take' is. Find a point in the extract where this device could be used to good comic effect.

6   Look carefully at the part Kate and Petruchio play in this scene. What do we learn of their individual characters and their relationship here? Re-read the last ten lines in particular. She calls him 'husband', but do they behave as husband and wife? Either rehearse this short section or discuss how it might be used to show a growing tenderness between the two of them.

Further development

1   Divide into groups of three. A is a lawyer who has been given the job of handing over a large inheritance to a dead millionaire's next-of-kin. B and C turn up both claiming that title. Improvise the scene in the lawyer's office as B and C try to convince A of their claims.

2   Your parents have gone away and left you in charge of the house, trusting you to keep an eye on things. You take this opportunity to have a party (just a little one!) but just as it is in full swing your parents unexpectedly return. Improvise the scene where they appear.

3   Kate and Petruchio have, until this point, had a stormy relationship. Perhaps it is in this scene that they discover, by watching the confused events taking place, that they have the same sense of humour and this leads them to develop more affection for each other. In pairs, improvise an argument between two people who have been forced by circumstances to live with each other. At some point a third person enters and does something that changes the atmosphere from tension to relief. Try to launch into this without planning but rely on your powers of invention to provide an idea on the spur of the moment.

4   With the help of your teacher, play a variation of the game 'Keeper of the Gate' to generate ideas on secrets. This might work as follows. The whole group sits in a semi-circle and one volunteer takes up position in the middle. It is her job to guard an imaginary door. Only she knows what is behind the door and she is anxious that no one else should find out. Students sitting in the semi-circle take it in turns to approach the doorkeeper and try to present a convincing argument as to why they should be let through and discuss what's inside. The doorkeeper must try to give logical and believable reasons not to allow them in. Whoever runs out of logical, reasonable arguments first is the loser.

5   Some of the ideas generated in Question 4 could help you to develop a scene in which each character has a secret which she is desperately trying to keep, although the situation is making it increasingly difficult for her to do so.

CANDLEFORD

by Keith Dewhurst

CAST (in order of appearance)

BEN

TOM

LAURA

MRS GUBBINS

BILL

SOLOMON

BAVOUR

BROWN

8 speaking parts. No doubling.

Candleford was first presented at the National Theatre in 1979 as the second half of a rather unusual project. The first half of the project had been presented a year earlier. Two plays were adapted from a trilogy of novels by Flora Thompson called *Lark Rise to Candleford*. The first play, simply called *Lark Rise*, takes place on the first day of the harvest. All the action takes place in the one day. Flora Thompson herself appears in the play as a little girl called Laura. In the second play, *Candleford*, Laura has grown old enough to go away to work in the post office and smithy of a neighbouring village. As *Lark Rise* is set on a hot summer's day, so *Candleford* is set on a cold winter's one. Both plays use folk songs to add to the atmosphere and make them more entertaining.

Making plays from novels isn't a particularly new idea. As you will probably know, many films are also made from original novels. *Lark Rise to Candleford* posed a tricky problem, though, in that there isn't really any story to it. The book is about different aspects of life in a small group of villages in Oxfordshire at the end of the twentieth century, and the reader's attention is kept not by the unfolding of a plot but by the colourful descriptions of the characters and their lives. The problem with dramatising such a book is that most pieces of theatre rely on 'dramatic tension' – the audience watches and listens because it wants to know what will happen next. With *Lark Rise to Candleford* a way had to be found of giving life to Flora Thompson's descriptions and recreating the atmosphere of village life. Most important, the audience would have to be made to feel a part of the village.

The style of the play

Keith Dewhurst's answer to the problem was to write the plays so that they could be performed as 'promenade productions' – that is to say that rather than having the audience seated looking forward onto a stage, or even having the action going on in the middle of the audience (theatre in the round) the audience are left to wander around with the action happening among them. Such a technique aimed to create an impression of life going on in the village just as Flora Thompson had described it, with the audience watching like invisible ghosts. Acting in a play like this requires enormous concentration on the part of the actors who have to make space for themselves and catch the audience's attention while trying to capture a sense of authenticity in the portrayal of their characters. Of course, from an audience's point of view, also, the experience is quite demanding as you have to keep moving around. Keith Dewhurst sums up the experience like this: 'No one sees all the play, although if it can be heard it can be followed, and some emotions must be read off the faces of other spectators. In a way each person is his or her own television camera, and at the same time part of the show.'

The extract

One of the post women, Mrs Macey, has been called away to attend to her sick husband. This gives the locals something to gossip about, as does the fact that today is the day of the hunt. The action takes place in and around the village post office, and while not very much actually happens the succession of local characters provides plenty of interest.

> BEN TROLLOPE *and* TOM ASHLEY *cross the green. They are old army pensioners.* BEN *is a tall, upright old fellow with a neat, well-brushed appearance and clear straight gaze.* TOM *is more retiring, a little shrunken, bent and wizened.*

BEN Pick your feet up, soldier. Pick 'em up.

TOM I'm freezin' cold.

BEN I know you're a-freezing, Tom. I know it. [*They enter the post office.*]

BEN   Afternoon, missy.   5

LAURA   Afternoon, Mr Trollope. Didn't expect to see you in this snow,
Mr Ashley.

TOM   Didn't expect to see myself.

LAURA   When were you here last?

TOM   Three month ago.   10

BEN   Last time us pensions were due. [*They present their books.* LAURA
checks them. There is money in the counter drawer.] Them's due again
today and I said today's the day we should collect 'em!

TOM   I said, 'Look here, I've got my mending and cooking to do', but
being the Sergeant he says, 'Quick march'.   15

LAURA   How's your garden in all this?

BEN   Geraniums and fuchsias is indoors; t'others takes their chance.
Interested in flowers, aren't you, missy?

LAURA   Oh, yes.

BEN   Aye.   20

LAURA   I like the way you line yours up, like soldiers.

TOM   That's what we was, missy!

BEN   Seeing as you like flowers you'd be head over heels with India,
wouldn't she, Tom, especially the Himalayas.

LAURA   Oh, but I know! Northward of the great plains of India, and   25
along the whole extent, towers and sublime mountain region of the
Himalayas, ascending gradually until it terminates in a long range of
summits wrapped in perpetual snow . . .

BEN   Have you learned that by heart?

LAURA   From a book at school.   30

BEN   Well, then, you deserve to go there yourself, for I never saw
anything like it, never in my life! Great sheets of scarlet as close-
packed as they grasses on the Green, and primulas and lilies and
things such as you only see here in a hothouse, and rising right out
of 'em, great mountains all covered with snow. Ah! 'Twas a sight –   35
a sight! And what scents, eh? What scents and smells! That's
why we rented our cottage – 'cause it had jessamine over the
door.

TOM   Aye. The scent of jessamine.

BEN   India, missy, India. I wake up sometimes and think I've heard the   40
bugle. I think I'll smell all the smells and blink my eyes in the glare
and see the mutineers come at us. Horsemen in the dust.

TOM   Sergeant. I want my mother, Sergeant.

BEN   Too late, son. Face your front and fire on the young gentleman's
command. [*Silence.* LAURA *watches them.*] Aye. Aye. It seems to get   45
hold of you, like, somehow. [LAURA *gives them their pension money.*]

Thank you, missy. Good day. [*Music starts, very quietly, as they go. Outside they check.*]

TOM   Imagine it; forty year ago a wench jilted me so I took the Queen's shilling. I'd not be that downcast now.   50

BEN   Haven't you left that curry on the hob?

TOM   Aye; and I wish we were back in India, with a bit of hot sun.

BEN   T'ain't no good wishing, Tom. We've had our day and that day's over. We shan't see India no more.

> BEN *and* TOM *sing their 'Old Soldier's Song'.* BEN *the first verse,* TOM *the second, both the chorus.*

Song   I left my native country   55
    I left my native home
    To wear a soldier's tunic
    And preserve the good Queen's throne.
    I travelled out to India, the mutiny to quell.
    I have visited sweet paradise, and seen the gates of hell.   60

Chorus   When we wore the scarlet and the blue,
    We took the old Queen's shilling
    When the Empire days were new.
    Forward into battle, don't you hear the bugle call.
    Raise the tattered standard and let me like a soldier fall.   65

    I've seen the Himalayas and I've been to Katmandu,
    Seen sights to dazzle Solomon,
    The tales I could tell you.
    From Banbury to Bombay,
    All the good times have gone by,   70
    Now don't believe the man who says, 'old soldiers never die'.

Chorus

> *They march off, as smartly as they can manage.* MRS GUBBINS *crosses the Green.* BILL, SOLOMON *and* BAVOUR *are passing in and out of the forge.*

BILL   Whoa-up, lads!

BAVOUR   Afternoon, Mrs Gubbins.

MRS GUBBINS   Huh!

SOLOMON [*singing*]   And huh say all of us!   75
    For she's a grumpy old sow like
    For she's a grumpy old sow like.

MRS GUBBINS [*arriving at the post office*]   No sign of the post yet?

LAURA   No.

MRS GUBBINS   Huh! Any news?   80

LAURA   News?

MRS GUBBINS   You know.

LAURA   I don't.

MRS GUBBINS   Mrs Macey.

LAURA   Oh . . .!   85

MRS GUBBINS   If there is, tell us now afore he comes.

LAURA   No. I mean there isn't. I mean, so far as I know there's been
no word. Wait a minute – here he is now.

POSTMAN BROWN *crosses the Green.*

BROWN   'Deep and wide . . .'

SMITHS   Praise the Lord. Jesus saves. Hallelujah.   90

BROWN *waves cheerily to the* SMITHS *and enters the post office.*

BROWN   Afternoon, young Laura.

LAURA   Afternoon, Mr Brown.

BROW   Mrs Gubbins.

MRS GUBBINS   Huh!

BROWN   How was your delivery?   95

LAURA   Fine.

BROWN   I knew you'd not flinch. [BROWN *emplies the postbag and they
set to work.*] Tell you what.

LAURA   What?

BROWN   As I was a-comin' up the Fordlow Lane, I see'd that there's   100
them old gippos again.

MRS GUBBINS   Gippos?

BROWN   Aye. Caravans and all!

MRS GUBBINS   Time they was routed out o'them places, the 'ole
stinkin' lot of 'em. If a poor man so much as looks at a rabbit he soon   105
finds hisself in quod but their pot's never empty.

BROWN   There's a lot of people says they eats hedgehogs! Hedgehogs!
He! He!

MRS GUBBINS   Hedgehogs! Ha! ha! ha!

BROWN   Hedgehogs wi' soft prickles!   110

MRS GUBBINS [*abruptly stops laughing*]   I seed that Mary Merton on the
Green.

BROWN   Eh?

MRS GUBBINS   There's summat there as is not as it should be.

BROWN   Wind's changed an' all. Come round to the West. I could   115 smell old Jolliffe's muckhill. [*They work.* BROWN *tries to keep his next remark sotto voce to* LAURA.] Any – er – any word from Mrs Macey?

MRS GUBBINS   What? What's that 'un said?

BROWN   Nothing.

MRS GUBBINS   Nothing?   120

BROWN   No.

MRS GUBBINS   Huh!

They work.

MRS GUBBINS [*she holds up a letter*]   Ha!

BROWN   Eh?

MRS GUBBINS   Look us here, now! Miss Mary Merton. To be called for   125
at the post office. Whose handwriting be that?

LAURA   I don't know.

MRS GUBBINS   Certain are you?

LAURA   Yes.

MRS GUBBINS   Huh!   130

They work.

BROWN   Mrs Gubbins.

MRS GUBBINS   Uh?

BROWN   How long have us knowed each other?

MRS GUBBINS   Twenty-five year.

BROWN   Thirty.   135

MRS GUBBINS   'Appen thirty.

BROWN   Aye, and I'll be jiggered if you've ever spoke very much,
except about other folk's business.

MRS GUBBINS   You can tell that to Jesus.

BROWN   I have found Jesus, Mrs Gubbins, [*Huge pause.*] and if I men-   140
tion you at all, I shall ask Him to help you, not tell tales about you.

MRS GUBBINS   Did you or did you not ask young Laura if 'un had heard
any word from Mrs Macey?

BROWN *opens his mouth to deny the charge and then realises that he
cannot.* MRS GUBBINS *chuckles.*

BROWN   I can't think what there is for you to laugh at.

MRS GUBBINS   You. Rain, hail, sunshine or snow, you're the biggest ole   145
gossip I've ever seed.

BROWN   I'm the – No, no! Not so. What it be is, that all sorts o'folk
confides in me.

MRS GUBBINS   Huh!

BROWN   Huh? Look 'ee 'ere. This very morning that Mrs Wardup   150 what lives at the hungry end of the Green taps on her window when she sees me, and my word, but haven't she got worries what with her sister's son not able to stop himself bed-wetting.

MRS GUBBINS Bed-wetting?

BROWN Aye. 155

MRS GUBBINS Fried mice.

BROWN Fried mice?

MRS GUBBINS Fried mice for the supper stops a growed man a-wetting his bed, never mind a nipper.

BROWN Fried mice. Well. I've never heard that one afore, have you, 160
young Laura?

MRS GUBBINS Huh. [*She sighs and shakes her head at them. She's not surprised. They work.* MRS GUBBINS *finds another interesting letter.*]

MRS GUBBINS Hello. Here's one for that Co-lo-nel.

LAURA Yes. Colonel Scott. 165

MRS GUBBINS Co-lo-nel.

LAURA Colonel.

MRS GUBBINS Co-lo-nel.

LAURA Colonel.

MRS GUBBINS Co-lo-nel as plain as the nose on your face. I don't 170
know what they teach 'em at school these days.

They work.

BROWN Mind you. I have heard of black slugs for warts.

MRS GUBBINS Slugs?

BROWN Slugs. For warts. You bind 'em on for a day and a night.

MRS GUBBINS Dead or alive? 175

BROWN The slugs? Alive. I saw it done once, twenty odd year ago, by a chap as sorted parcels at Candleford. [*They work.*] Mind you; when he took the slug off it were dead.

MRS GUBBINS What about the wart?

BROWN Well, no more'n a week after, the young chap's transfer came 180
through. General Post Office, Oxford. I never seed him again.

MRS GUBBINS But did 'un, or did 'un not, charm the wart?

BROWN Dunno, do I? He still had 'un when he left Candleford.

MRS GUBBINS *sighs.*

BROWN Is this 'ere, all the village delivery?

MRS GUBBINS Aye. 185

LAURA Yes.

BROWN I'll be off with 'un then – and come back with the letter-box post. [*On his way out* BROWN *checks.*] You'll notice it's a-thawed a bit.

MRS GUBBINS   Eh?

BROWN   I said you'll notice it's thawed a bit. Allus the same. I'm jig-   190
gered if it's not. Thaws, and just starts to freeze again afore the afternoon delivery. [*Sings.*] 'Yes, Jesus loves me . . .'

> As BROWN *passes the forge the men are finishing their work. They sing*
> *as they go into the living room for their tea. It is almost dark again.*
> *Lamps are lit . . .*

Understanding the text

1   List five things that you find out about Ben and Tom through what they say
in this scene. For example, we know they are pensioners because they have come
to collect their pensions.

2   Part of the playwright's art is to be able to tell an audience not only about
the characters in the way you discovered in Question 1, but something about the
time and place in which they exist. Pick out three things which are said which
show that:
   *   the play is set in the country
   *   it is not in the present day.
What other bits of information are included in the dialogue here which you think
are important for the audience's understanding?

3   There are a number of touches of gentle humour in the scene which give the
characters a warmth and make them believable. Pick out any lines that you feel
achieve this particularly well. It might be interesting for you to compare the characterisation of rural folk here to that in *The Body*.

4   Look at the discussion between Laura and Mrs Gubbins about how to pro-
nounce the word Colonel. What does this tell us about Laura?

Producing the scene

1   List the different locations mentioned in the scene. Imagine you are producing this play in your school hall. Draw a sketch or diagram showing how you
could use its full space to recreate the village and suggest both the inside and
outside of the post office and smithy. Bear in mind that the audience, in promenade performance, can move around but as many as possible should be able to
watch each different scene.

2   Suggest as many ways as you can of creating the atmosphere of a really cold
day. What techniques could the actors use to help the audience also feel a part

of this cold day? With the help of your teacher divide the class into two groups. Group A should imagine that they have come to watch this play. Group B, as the actors, enter and improvise with Group A to establish the location and the idea of a cold day. What can you say and do to create the scene within a short space of time?

3   Design a costume for either Tom, Ben or Laura and give reasons for your choice of clothes.

4   Imagine you are playing either Brown or Mrs Gubbins. Describe what sort of person you think he/she is and explain how you could use your voice and body to recreate them.

5   Why do you think Tom suddenly says, 'Sergeant. I want my mother, Sergeant,' to which Ben replies, 'Too late, son. Face your front and fire on the young gentleman's command'? What suggestions would you give the actors about how to deliver these lines? Act out this short extract and try to change the atmosphere from that of the post office to that of the front line by changing tone of voice and position.

6   What reasons can you give for the inclusion of the 'Old Soldier's Song'? Given that in a promenade performance the actors are working in among the audience consider:

- what problems this might pose for the actors playing Tom and Ben
- how they could stage the song so as actively to help the audience feel the atmosphere of the song's lyrics.

Further development

1   Laura's family live in a neighbouring village. In pairs or small groups, act out a scene in which she goes to visit them. What news would she take from Candleford?

2   As well as being gossips, Brown and Mrs Gubbins have some interesting ideas about medicine. Set up a scene in a hospital which specialises in using 'traditional' cures for ailments. Be as bizarre and imaginative as you like.

3   Bill, Solomon and Bavour are apprentice smiths in the village. Most of their work on this day has come from the local gentry who are off hunting. Write or improvise a scene which shows how the smiths would talk and behave to the hunters.

4   The post office seems to be a good place to catch up on local gossip and meet a cross-section of the local people. Can you suggest any other places in the village which might also be good for 'studying' the locals? Set up an improvisation in such a place and see if, bit by bit, you can invent your own colourful personalities.

5   Imagine that, at some point, Laura and the others in this scene have their photograph taken. In groups position yourselves to show the relationship

between the characters and, as far as possible, their characters and attitudes. Extend the photograph to include other villagers either mentioned in the play or of your own invention. If each character were allowed to say one line about their life in Candleford, what would it be?

6   The play has a strong air of nostalgia about it. Ben and Tom talk about their former lives in India, and life in the village is depicted as being straightforward and enjoyable. Have you ever heard older people going on about 'the good old days'? What sort of things do they say? Think about your own area, town or village and in small groups act out a scene in which a number of old people are reminiscing about days gone by.

7   Following on from Question 6, look carefully at the extract and see if you can find anything that suggests that life in a village a hundred years ago may actually have been quite hard. You could do some research of your own into what life was like in your home town in, say, your grandparents' time. See if you can make a piece of theatre that shows that people sometimes think 'the good old days' were better than they actually were. Perhaps your scene could aim to remind them of the real hardships faced.

TWO WEEKS WITH THE QUEEN

by Mary Morris

CAST (in order of appearance)

IRIS

BOB

ALISTAIR

COLIN

TED

WOMAN

*BUSINESSMAN

LUKE

*MUM

*DAD

7 speaking parts. *Non-speaking parts.

Two Weeks with the Queen started life as a short novel written by Morris Gleitzman. It tells the story of twelve-year-old Colin Mudford who is sent to England from his Australian home when his younger brother Luke becomes ill with leukaemia. Colin's parents think that it will be best for him not to be there to see his brother die so they arrange for him to stay with his mother's sister in London. Colin decides that going to London will give him the chance of contacting the Queen herself and persuading her to send her best doctor to cure Luke. He enlists the help of his rather wimpish cousin Alistair to help him with this project. As a result he gets into a number of scrapes which don't go down at all well with his well-meaning but desperately narrow-minded aunt and uncle, Bob and Iris. Taking matters into his own hands, Colin visits a hospital in search of a good doctor and meets up with Ted, whose partner Griff is dying of AIDS. As their friendship develops, Ted draws strength from Colin's innocent faith and good humour. Colin is with Ted and Griff when Griff dies and this helps him to accept that Luke will die also. The experience makes him realise that his parents were wrong to send him away and that the best thing for Luke will be to be with him when he dies.

Despite its tragic theme, *Two Weeks with the Queen* is a very funny play which ultimately makes the audience feel good. It manages this mainly through the character of Colin whose enthusiasm for life and determination not to give in to tragedy is a lesson for all the adults he encounters. His aunt and uncle, Bob and Iris, are embarrassed by the situation and can't even bear to hear the word 'cancer' let alone know how to deal with the fact that Ted is gay and Griff has AIDS. Colin, though, takes people as he finds them. He says what he means and completely rejects anything that smacks of hypocrisy or cruelty. The key to Colin's development is in his realisation that adults can be, and frequently are, wrong. This understanding is his gift to his cousin Alistair who, at the end of the play, starts to stand up to his parents.

The style of the play

In many ways, *Two Weeks with the Queen* is like a television drama in that it quickly switches from one short scene to the next. Although the play touches on a number of serious issues, such as how to deal with death and gay relationships, it doesn't explore these in any depth. Rather, each new scene is a stepping stone in Colin's story. Apart from Colin, and to some extent Ted, the characters are little more than stereotypes whose dramatic function is to move the story along, leaving the audience to think about the underlying issues for themselves. Performing the play requires the actors to work at a cracking pace so, while the scenes take place in a number of different locations, there isn't time for elaborate set changes. While television dramas have the luxury of cutting from one place to another in a split second, a stage performance of this play means trusting the dialogue and the actions to put the audience in the picture.

The extract

Colin has tried to contact the Queen in a number of ways. He has written to her but received no reply. He has even tried to break into Buckingham Palace to see her personally but simply got arrested! His visit to a top London hospital ends with him being thrown out by a snotty consultant, but as a result of this he meets Ted. This extract is the last section of the play. Following Griff's death, Colin invites Ted to his aunt's and uncle's house in the hope of giving him some comfort. Their inability to know what to say or do in the face of loss convinces Colin he must go back to his brother. Knowing that his aunt and uncle won't allow him to do this, he gets Ted to help him. His plan is nearly scuppered at the airport when Bob and Iris turn up to stop him, but it is his cousin Alistair who finally makes them see the sense of letting Colin go home.

IRIS *wheels a tea trolley in,* BOB *places some chairs around.* ALISTAIR *joins them and they sit formally.* ALISTAIR *reaches for a biscuit from the trolley,* IRIS *slaps his hand. A kitch doorbell is heard and they jump up in apprehension.* COLIN *tears out of the room in his usual bullet-fashion.*

COLIN   I'll get it! [*He returns with* TED.] Auntie Iris, Uncle Bob, this is my mate, Ted. The one with his mouth hangin' open is my cousin Alistair.

ALISTAIR *shuts his mouth, there are 'pleased-to-meet yous' all round.* TED *is sat down. They all look at each other smiling stiffly and then all say something at once.*

IRIS   Cup of tea, Ted?

TED   Thank you. [IRIS *starts to pour,* ALISTAIR *grabs the opportunity to* 5 *take a biscuit.*] Nice home you have.

IRIS   Thank you Ted. Bob's a bit of a do-it-yourself enthusiast.

BOB   Only way. I'm not paying hundreds of pounds to some cowboy to mess up my plumbing, eh?

TED   Quite right. 10

BOB   You into home improvements?

TED   Er, no, not much.

IRIS   The biggest hardware centre in Greater London's not far from here. Bob could show you around.

TED   Another time perhaps. 15

BOB   What do you do for a crust, Ted?

TED   I'm unemployed.

COLIN   He's not a dole-bludger. He had to stay home and look after Griff.

TED *looks like he is going to cry. His teacup starts to wobble. He puts it on the trolley.*

IRIS   Top up, Ted? [*He shakes his head.*] Biscuit? Piece of cake? 20

Suddenly IRIS *picks up a bowl from the trolley. She hands it round (missing* ALISTAIR*). Everybody takes a tangerine.*

They're lovely, these. Take your mind off . . . things.

TED *begins to cry.* IRIS *motions to* BOB *to take* ALISTAIR *out of the room. He does so. There is silence as* TED *cries.* COLIN *is struggling not to cry too.* TED *pulls himself together a little.*

[*Kindly.*] Would you like your cup of tea now, love?

TED *tries to answer, but he cannot.* COLIN, *his voice very shaky, answers for him.*

COLIN   He'll be right, thanks.
TED [*to* COLIN]   I think I'd better go. [*To* IRIS.] Thanks very much.
IRIS   You don't have to go, love. Stay until you feel better.   25
TED   No, I'll be alright now.
IRIS   Are you sure?
TED   Thank you, yes.
IRIS   Alright, take care of yourself then.
TED   Thanks.   30
IRIS   Bye then.

COLIN *sees* TED *off.* IRIS *studies the tangerines, puzzled.* COLIN *re-enters. He stands looking at his aunty* IRIS. *He starts to cry.*

COLIN   I want to go home.
IRIS   Oh pet.

IRIS *holds out her arms.* COLIN *runs to her and cries in her arms loud and long. As he quietens,* BOB *and* ALISTAIR *return.*

BOB   Alright, then?
IRIS   He's alright, aren't you love?   35
COLIN   Yeh.
IRIS   Bit homesick, that's all.
COLIN   It's not just that. I've got to go home.
IRIS   You will, love, when things are . . . you know.
COLIN   I don't understand. I have to go home and be with Luke.   40
IRIS   You can't love.
BOB   You don't really want to go back to all that, do you?
COLIN   Yes.
IRIS   No you don't.
ALISTAIR   Yes he does.   45
IRIS   Shut up, Alistair.
COLIN   I got to go, auntie.
ALISTAIR   See.
BOB   You heard your mother, Alistair.
COLIN   Please.   50
ALISTAIR   Go on, let him.

BOB *points out of the room and* ALISTAIR *shuffles off.* BOB *gives him a hurry-up and follows.*

COLIN   You can't stop me. I have to go home!

IRIS Now listen to me, love, put it out of your mind, you can't go home. You'll understand when you're older that it's for the best.

COLIN No! You're wrong!   55

IRIS Now stop this nonsense.

COLIN I told you, I'm going home!

IRIS Listen to me Colin. I'm sorry things are so hard for you love, but you're not going to Australia, and that's that. And just in case you and Alistair have got any notions of cooking something up, don't   60
waste your time. They won't let you on the plane without a guardian to sign the forms. Now, I don't want to hear another word about it. OK? OK??

COLIN OK. I won't mention it again.

IRIS There's a good lad.   65

At the airport. There is a small counter with a WOMAN *behind it.* TED *paces up and down.* COLIN *enters lugging his suitcase.*

TED I thought you weren't going to make it.

COLIN Yeh, took me a while to figure out how to get the new lock off.

TED Nobody woke up, then?

COLIN Snoring their heads off.

TED Better get checked in.   70

They go to the desk. The WOMAN *takes* COLIN's *case and his ticket.*

WOMAN Travelling alone?

COLIN Yes.

WOMAN [*to* TED] What relationship are you to the traveller?

COLIN Mate.

TED Friend.   75

WOMAN Guardian?

COLIN That's right.

WOMAN Sign here please, so the young man can travel unaccompanied. [TED *sighs.*]

TED [*they walk away from the desk*] Well, this is it then.   80

COLIN I hope you don't get into trouble, signing and stuff.

TED Nah. Besides, I'm used to trouble. Think about me sometimes . . . and Griff.

COLIN I got you a present. Here. [COLIN *digs in his pocket and hands* TED *a pink scarf.*]   85

TED Great! My favourite colour.

They hug. TED *puts the scarf on and flips it over his shoulder.*

See ya Colin.

COLIN   See ya Ted.

TED *leaves.*
AUNTIE IRIS *and* UNCLE BOB *rush in.* ALISTAIR *puffs up behind.*

IRIS   STOP! Stop that boy!
COLIN   Shit!   90

COLIN *makes a run for it. They all try to grab him, including the air-port* WOMAN, *there is much tripping up and tangling (some of it done by* ALISTAIR *who is on* COLIN's *side). Finally, they collar him.*

WOMAN   Alright, now what is going on here?
IRIS   This young man is trying to leave the country illegally.
COLIN   No I'm not. I'm an Australian citizen, I got my passport and I'm going home!
IRIS   You're an under-age Australian citizen and you're not going any-   95
where!
WOMAN   Who exactly are you people?
BOB   I'm this boy's Uncle, he's under my care.
WOMAN   You're his guardian?
BOB   Legal guardian I am.   100
WOMAN   But what about the man who signed the form?
IRIS   Who signed? Colin, who was it? Was it your friend Ted? He's in big trouble my lad, big trouble.
WOMAN   I'd better get the airport police.
COLIN   No! The police don't like him, please don't.   105
BOB   That won't be necessary, thank you very much. There's no real harm done. We'll sort things out.
IRIS   Now then Colin. We're going to have no more . . .
COLIN   The plane'll be leaving in a minute. Let me go, please?
ALISTAIR   I think you should let him.   110
IRIS   Shut up Alistair.
ALISTAIR   No, really . . .
BOB   You heard your mother.
COLIN   I've got to go.
IRIS   I'm warning you Colin Mudford . . .   115
COLIN   I'm going. You can't watch me every minute of the day and night! If you lock me up I'll escape . . .
ALISTAIR   He will, you know.
BOB and IRIS   SHUT UP Alistair!
COLIN   I'll get home somehow.   120
BOB   Come on Colin lad, don't you think we've had enough of all this?

ALISTAIR [*yelling*]   Enough! I'll tell you who's had enough! I've had enough, that's who's had enough! [*Stunned silence.*] I've got him thinking up all sorts of tricks to get me into trouble and you telling   125
me what to do night and day. Do this Alistair, do that! Well I've had it! What makes you grown-ups so smart that you know what's best for everybody? You're not smart at all, any of you! He's the one that knows what's best for him and Luke, not you! He knows where he wants to be and he's goin' and that's final! [*Silence.*]   130

IRIS   Alistair . . .?

ALISTAIR [*losing his bottle*]   Sorry . . .

IRIS   Bob, our Alistair's growing up. Oh, Alistair.

BOB   Yes, well . . .

IRIS   Maybe the boy's got a point.   135

COLIN   Please . . .

IRIS   What do you think Bob?

There is a last boarding call announcement. BOB *ponders.*

BOB   Let the lad go home.

IRIS   I don't know what I'm going to say to your mother.

COLIN   Mum'll be right.   140

IRIS   Well . . . be off with you then.

COLIN   I love you auntie Iris.

IRIS   Oh, stop that.

COLIN   Onya Alistair. Oh, here, I meant to give you this. [*He gives* ALISTAIR *his Swiss army knife.*] You might need it one day.   145

ALISTAIR   Aw, brill!

IRIS   Alistair, give that back. You'll cut yourself.

ALISTAIR   No I won't.

IRIS   Oh. Well be careful with it then. Look after yourself Colin, love.

ALISTAIR [*getting a letter out*]   I nearly forgot. The postman brought   150
this for you. It's from Buckingham Palace.

COLIN *opens the letter and reads aloud.*

COLIN   Dear Mr Mudford. Her Majesty's sympathies are with all who suffer through illness. May I, on her behalf, wish your brother a speedy recovery. Signed . . . I can't read the signature . . . Palace Li . . .   155

ALISTAIR [*he had read it*]   Palace Liaison Officer – oops!

BOB   Her Majesty's sympathies! Huh!

COLIN [*screwing the letter up and throwing it at* ALISTAIR *and mimicking* BOB]   Get me started on the Queen!

ALISTAIR [*drop-kicking it back*]   Ought to be stuffed and put in a   160
museum!

BOB   Too right! Say hello to everyone for us Colin.

COLIN   Yeh, see ya. [*They kiss him.*]

ALISTAIR   See ya Colin.

They wave. COLIN *waves back.*

ALISTAIR [*to* BOB]   They're charging by the minute in that car park . . .   165
Eh Dad?

BOB   Right son.

They hurry off toward the car park. The last call for COLIN*'s plane is heard.*

LOUDSPEAKER VOICE   Now boarding from gate number ten is Qantas flight number two to Sydney via Singapore and Melbourne. This is your last call, your last call for Qantas flight number two to Sydney   170
via Singapore and Melbourne.

The BUSINESSMAN *from the flight over hurries on, he is busy checking his ticket and does not notice* COLIN.

COLIN   G'day! Fancy meeting you again!

The BUSINESSMAN *looks at* COLIN *in horror.*

What number's your ticket? Let's have a look. Hey, you've got the seat next to me again. Where you goin'?

The BUSINESSMAN *backs away, shaking his head. He turns and runs off, waving his ticket.*

You'll miss the plane! Poor bugger must have indigestion again.   175

COLIN *heads for the plane.*

LUKE *is in his hospital bed.* MUM *and* DAD *sit beside him.* COLIN *enters.* LUKE *sits up and flings his arms wide.*

LUKE   Colin! Colin! Colin!

MUM *and* DAD *look up. Their faces light up.* COLIN *rushes into* LUKE*'s arms.*

THE END

Understanding the text

1   A famous director once said that there is no such thing as a small part – only small actors! What he was suggesting, of course, is that even if a character only appears fleetingly on the stage and says little or nothing, there is still a reason for them being there. Divide a sheet of paper into two columns. In the first column list all of the characters in this extract which appear only to have a minor part. In the second column, explain why each one of them is nevertheless important and helps to move the story on in some way or helps an audience understand more about one of the major characters.

2   Do you think that Bob and Iris come across as 'real' people or are they more like stereotypes? Pick out examples of things they do and say to support your impression of them.

3   Although Colin is only twelve years old, he seems to make quite an impact on other people's lives. Pick two of the other characters that appear in this extract and describe how knowing Colin changes them. Pick out at least two lines of dialogue for each of these characters as evidence of Colin's effect on them.

4   *Two Weeks with the Queen* touches on some pretty heavy issues. Although these are not openly discussed in depth, the audience is left in no doubt that the main characters are thinking about them and feel deeply about their situation. Pick out at least three lines or incidents which suggest to you that what a character says is just the tip of the iceberg when it comes to what they are feeling inside.

5   What do you suppose the various characters in the play think about Colin? As a whole group, stand in a circle and place an empty chair in the middle to represent Colin. Each of you should think of a character that knows Colin (this would include his own mum and dad, Luke and even the businessman). Think of a line that your chosen character might at some point say to Colin and take turns going up to the chair and delivering the line as if it were to his face. Repeat the exercise, only this time think of a line that your character would say to someone else *about* Colin. Talk about the different attitudes that come out of this exercise. For example, his Aunty Iris might always appear to be telling him off to his face but might tell other people how much she really admires him for being so brave (on the other hand, you might decide that she would say that he really doesn't understand how bad the situation is).

6   Although this play tackles the sad business of losing people who are close to you, in what way do you think it can also be justifiably described as having a 'feel good factor'?

Producing the scene

1   In some ways *Two Weeks with the Queen* is like a television drama in that it snaps from one scene to the next very quickly. This is quite demanding on the

actors who must be able to change the mood of their character in an instant. It also presents a challenge for the design team. Changing elaborate, detailed sets for each new scene would slow the pace of the play down. Divide a sheet of paper into five columns with the headings: 'Setting, Props, Stage furniture, Lighting, Sound effects' and jot down ways of suggesting the different locations in this extract quickly and simply.

2   In groups, rehearse the scene in which Ted comes for tea. You need to remember that all Bob and Iris know about Ted is that he is gay and that his partner has just died of AIDS. Not a great deal is said during the scene but try to find things for the actors to do on stage that would emphasise that they are trying to be sociable but find the situation awkward and embarrassing.

3   Colin and Alistair are clearly two very different characters. How could this be suggested in the costumes they wear?

4   Alistair in particular seems to change a great deal through the play and this begins to become more apparent in this extract. Pick three moments from the extract – one from the start, one from the middle and one towards the end. Working in pairs, one of you should play Alistair and allow your working partner to 'model' you at these three moments. Try out different ways of sitting/ standing and different facial expressions that would illustrate how Alistair's character develops through the extract.

Further development

1   We can deduce from Colin's line 'G'day! Fancy meeting you again!' that he has met the businessman before. Improvise a scene which would explain why the businessman would rather miss his flight to Australia than spend any more time in Colin's company.

2   Write or improvise a scene in which Colin persuades Alistair to help him in his plan to recruit the Queen's top doctor to cure his brother Luke. What might the plan involve? How does Colin go about persuading Alistair to help him? What happens when they put the plan into action?

3   We have all no doubt found ourselves in situations where we don't really know what to say. In groups, think up just such a situation and improvise it in two contrasting ways:

  • In the first example, look for ways of playing the scene for laughs by having characters saying inappropriate things, then perhaps realising to their horror what they have just said. Maybe they make the situation worse by trying to dig themselves out of the hole they have put themselves into.

  • Try the same scenario again, but this time deliberately set out to make the audience share the characters' discomfort and really feel for them.

Talk about what you had to do as actors to achieve the two effects. Which scene was: (a) easiest to play; (b) had the most dramatic impact? Can you say why?

4   Imagine that Colin's mum and dad had a photo album of their two sons. In pairs, devise a series of still images that would show their life together and their developing relationship. You might choose to put a caption to each image and perhaps choose a piece of music that would add to the dramatic effect of the collage when it is presented.

5   Working on your own or in pairs, write a letter from Colin to Ted after Luke's death, then write Ted's reply. It would be interesting to find a way of presenting these on stage; would you have the character reading aloud what they are writing as they are writing it? Or would it be better to have them reading aloud the letter they had received? Perhaps it would be effective to mix both methods and cut from one character to the other.

Activity chart

The chart on pages 168–169 shows the skills that are developed in the activities section of each extract. Across the top of the chart are the extract titles, in order. Down the side are fifteen of the main assessment criteria for Drama at first examinations.

You can use the chart as a quick reference aid. With it you can:

• find a particular activity;
• plan longer coursework or project investigations based on particular areas of your syllabus;
• identify the types of activities developed with particular extracts.

The chart is especially helpful if you want to pursue a particular line of investigation, for example costume design. Read across the 'Costume design' line and you will find all the extracts with activities to help you in your investigation.

The chart is also helpful if you are stuck on a particular activity. It enables you to find similar activities which will help clarify or develop your work.

Finally the chart is helpful if you want to know which extracts to select for particular areas of work in Drama.

In the chart the following abbreviations are used:

UT   Understanding the text
PS   Producing the scene
FD   Further development.

So, UT 3/4 in the square for Characterisation under *Vinegar Tom* shows that activities 3 and 4 in the 'Understanding the text' section of *Vinegar Tom* all involve work on characterisation.

	Marigolds	Example	Indians	The Visit	She's Dead	Johnson over Jordan	The Gut Girls	The Lucky Ones
Characterisation	UT 1/2/3 FD 3/5	UT 2	UT 3 PS 6	UT 3 FD 7	PS 6 FD 6	UT 2/3 PS 4 FD 2	UT 1/4	UT 1/3
Use of language	UT 4/6	UT 1	UT 1/2/4		UT 2/3/4 FD 5/6		UT 2/3	UT 2
Theatrical style		UT 3/4	UT 5	UT 1/4	UT 1	UT 1/4		UT 4
Set/props design	PS 1	PS 1/2	PS 1/3		PS 1/2		PS 1/2	PS 1
Lighting and sound	PS 1/6	PS 3	PS 4			PS 1/2/3 FD 7		
Costume design	PS 2		PS 2	PS 1		PS 4		
Movement work	FD 4	FD 4	PS 6	PS 3/5/7		PS 5	PS 5	PS 5 FD 7
Vocal work	PS 4/7			PS 2/4/5	PS 5/7/8	FD 5		PS 2
Directing acting	PS 3/4/5	PS 4	PS 5	PS 2	PS 4/5	PS 6/7	PS 4/5	PS 4
Stage direction	PS 5		PS 6/7	PS 5	PS 3/7/8	PS 7	PS 2/4/5	PS 3
Spontaneous improvisation	FD 1/2/6	FD 1	FD 2/3	FD 1/4/6	FD 1/2/3	FD 1/2/3/4	FD 3/4	FD 1/2/3
Prepared improvisation	FD 3/5	FD 2/3	FD 4/5/6	FD 2/3/5	FD 4/7	FD 6	FD 1/2/5	FD 4/5/6
Script/ creative writing	FD 7	PS 6 FD 3	FD 4/5/6	FD 4	FD 6	FD 3/6	FD 5	FD 5/6
Discussion		FD 4	FD 1	UT 2	UT 5 FD 4		UT 5	PS 6 FD 6/7
Research		FD 2/4	FD 6	UT 2			PS 3	

Vinegar Tom	Black Comedy	The Golden Pathway Annual	The Body	The Taming of the Shrew	Candleford	Two Weeks with the Queen
UT 3/4	UT 1/3/5	UT 4 PS 4 FD 3	UT 2/3/4	UT 1/3	UT 1/4 PS 4 FD4/5	UT 1/2/3/4/5 PS 4
UT 1		UT 1	UT 1/4	UT 2/4		UT 2/3
UT 3/5 PS 3	UT 1/2/4/6	UT 3 FD 7	UT 5	UT 5	UT 2/3	UT 4/6 PS1
PS 1/2	PS 1		PS 3/4	PS 1/2	PS 1	PS 1
	PS 3		PS 5/8		PS 2/5/6	PS 1 FD 4
	PS 2	PS 4	PS 1/2		PS 3	PS 3
	PS 4	PS 3	PS 6		FD 5	PS4 FD 4
PS 3/7 FD 7			FD 1/2			
PS 4	PS 3	PS 1/2	PS 7	PS 4/5/6		PS 2/4
PS 6 FD 6	PS 4	PS 5/6		PS 2/3		PS 2
FD 1/3	FD 1/2	FD 2/3/5	FD 3	FD 1/2/3/4	FD 1/2	FD 1
FD 3/4/5	FD 3/4	FD 1/4/6	FD 4/5	FD 5/6	FD 3/6/7	FD 2/3/5
FD 3/4/7		FD 6	FD 2	FD 6	FD 6/7	FD 2/5
		FD 6	FD 5			UT 6
	UT 6				FD 6/7	

Key
UT — Understanding the text
PS — Producing the scene
FD — Further development

169

Acknowledgements

The authors and publishers wish to thank the following for permission to reproduce copyright material in this book:

Reproduced by permission of Methuen Publishing Limited:
 Extract from 'The Body' from *Darke Plays 1* by Nick Darke
 Extract from 'Example' from *Theatre-in-Education Programmes: Secondary*, edited by Pam Schweitzer
 Extract from 'The Gut Girls' from *Daniels Plays 2* by Sarah Daniels
 Extract from *Indians* by Arthur Kopit
 Extract from 'The Lucky Ones' from *Welcome Home, Raspberry, The Lucky Ones: Three Plays* by Tony Marchant
 Extract from 'She's Dead' from *Tests* by Paul Ableman
 Extract from 'Vinegar Tom' from *Churchill Plays 1* by Caryl Churchill.

Extract from *Two Weeks with the Queen* by Mary Morris (1994) published by Macmillan Publishers Ltd.

Extract from *The Visit* by Friedrich Durrenmatt published by Jonathan Cape. Used by permission of Random House Group Limited.

Extract from *Black Comedy* © Peter Shaffer 1967. Used by permission of London Management.

Extract from *The Golden Pathway Annual* by John Harding and John Burrows. Used by permission of Alan Brodie Representation Ltd.

Every effort has been made to contact copyright holders. The publishers apologise to anyone whose rights have been inadvertently overlooked, and will be happy to rectify any errors or omissions.